The Lord's Prayer Devotional

Deepening in the Most Well-Known Prayer

David H. Kim

ISBN: 0984730613
ISBN-13: 978-0984730612

To my loving parents whose lifestyle of prayer
has modeled for me the power
of persistent and faithful prayer.

TABLE OF CONTENTS

PREFACE: HOW TO USE THIS DEVOTIONAL

When people ask me what's the best way to learn how pray to God, the simplest and most profound place to point people towards is the Lord's Prayer found in Matthew 6:9-13 and Luke 11:1-4 in the Bible. In these short verses, Jesus himself teaches his disciples how to pray. For this reason, most Christians have committed to memory these verses at one time in their lives; however, the Lord's Prayer was meant to be so much more than a rote prayer to be memorized. Hidden within these short verses is a rich Biblical tapestry that unlocks the depth and meaning of each petition. When we grasp this larger Biblical context, we begin to appreciate the richness of this prayer and the way it brings us into closer fellowship with God. Above all, this prayer realigns us to the gospel and what Christ has accomplished for us.

There are a total of 20 devotionals which are meant to done within the context of one month (5 devotionals a week). The purpose of this devotional is three fold: 1) to understand the larger Biblical context of the Lord's Prayer, 2) to learn how to deepen in prayer both in terms of substance as well as duration, and 3) to introduce some helpful resources that will continue the learning process. There are a total of twenty devotionals that I recommend to be completed (best in a group) over the course of 4 weeks (Mon-Fri). You will see that the format of each day changes depending on the petition, and the duration of prayer will increase with each passing week. You will encounter Scripture, extra-Biblical resources, and questions to guide you in the processing of the petitions. I would encourage all those who go through this devotional to commit 30-60 minutes a day and to use a journal to record the progression of your thoughts and times with the Lord. Certain days require more time to process than you might have, so feel free to return to those days so that you don't feel so rushed to complete it.

As you journey through this book, my prayer is that it will lead you to see the beauty, depth, and privilege of what Jesus taught his disciples millennia ago. There is an intimacy with Christ hidden in this prayer that I hope will become increasingly yours as the weeks progress.

DAY 1: THE SIN OF PRAYERLESSNESS

Before we dive into the actual content of the Lord's Prayer, it's helpful to first reflect upon the things that block our prayer lives from growing. Many can readily admit to the lack of prayer in their lives, but few connect this omission to sin. No one would say not praying is as bad as murder or theft, but to have this view is to misunderstand the role of prayer in the believer's life. As we begin this devotional series, we have to first understand how prayerlessness is a manifestation of unbelief in our hearts. As Romans 14:23 states, "For whatever does not proceed from faith is sin."

We will be reading today and tomorrow two excerpts from *The Believer's Prayer Life* by Andrew Murray (1828-1917) who was a South African writer, teacher, and pastor.

. . .

The Sin of Prayerlessness

If conscience is to do its work, and the contrite heart is to feel its misery, it is necessary that each individual should mention his sin by name. The confession must be severely personal. In a meeting of ministers there is probably no single sin, which each one of us ought to acknowledge with deeper shame — 'Guilty, verily guilty'—than the sin of prayerlessness.

What is it, then, that makes prayerlessness such a great sin? At first it is looked upon merely as a weakness. There is so much talk about lack of time and all sorts of distractions that the deep guilt of the situation is not recognized. Let it be our honest desire that, for the future, the sin of prayerlessness may be to us truly sinful. Consider:

1. WHAT A REPROACH IT IS TO GOD.

There is the holy and most glorious God who invites us to come to him, to hold converse with him, to ask from him such things as we need, and to experience what a blessing there is in fellowship with him. He has created us in his own image, and has redeemed us by His own Son so that in converse with Him we might find our highest glory and salvation.

What use do we make of this heavenly privilege? How many there are who take only five minutes for prayer! They say that they have no time and that the heart's desire for prayer is lacking; they do not know how to spend half an hour with God! It is not that they absolutely do not pray; they pray every day—but they have no joy in prayer, as a token of communion with God which shows that God is everything to them.

If a friend comes to visit them, they have time, they make time, even at the cost of sacrifice, for the sake of enjoying converse with him. Yes, they have time for everything that really interests them, but no time to practice fellowship with God and delight themselves in him! They find time for a creature who can be of service to them; but day after day, month after month passes, and there is no time to spend one hour with God.

Do not our hearts begin to acknowledge what a dishonor, what a despite of God this is, that I dare to say I cannot find time for fellowship with him? If this sin begins to appear plain to us, shall we not with deep shame cry out: 'Woe is me, for I am undone, O God; be merciful to me, and forgive this awful sin of prayerlessness.' Consider further:

2. IT IS THE CAUSE OF A DEFICIT SPIRITUAL LIFE.

It is a proof that, for the most part, our life is still under the power of 'the flesh'. Prayer is the pulse of life; by it the doctor can tell what is the condition of the heart. The sin of prayerlessness is a proof for the ordinary Christian or minister that the life of God in the soul is in deadly sickness and weakness.

Much is said and many complaints are made about the feebleness of the Church to fulfill her calling, to exercise an influence over her members, to deliver them from the power of the world, and to bring them to a life of holy consecration to God. Much is also spoken about her indifference to the millions of heathen whom Christ entrusted to her that she might make known to them his love and salvation. What is the reason that many thousands of Christian workers in the world have not a greater influence? Nothing save this—the prayerlessness of their service. In the midst of all their zeal in the study and in the work of the Church, of all their faithfulness in preaching and conversation with the people, they lack that ceaseless prayer which has attached to it the sure promise of the Spirit and the power from on high. It is nothing but the sin of prayerlessness which is the cause of the lack of a powerful spiritual life! Consider further:

3. THE DREADFUL LOSS WHICH THE CHURCH SUFFERS AS A RESULT OF THE PRAYERLESSNESS OF THE MINISTER.

It is the business of a minister to train believers up to a life of prayer; but how can a leader do this if he himself understands little the art of conversing with God and of receiving from the Holy Spirit, every day, out of heaven, abundant grace for himself and for his work? A minister cannot lead a congregation higher than he is himself. He cannot with enthusiasm point out a way, or explain a work, in which he is not himself walking or living.

How many thousands of Christians there are who know next to nothing of the blessedness of prayer and fellowship with God! How many there are who know something of it and long for a further increase of this knowledge, but in the preaching of the Word they are not persistently urged to keep on till they obtain the blessing! The reason is simply and only that the minister understands so little about the secret of powerful prayer and does not give prayer the place in his service which, in the nature of the case and in the will of God, is indispensably necessary. Oh, what a difference we should notice in our congregations if ministers could be brought to see in its right light the sin of prayerlessness and were delivered from it! Once more consider:

4. THE IMPOSSIBILITY OF PREACHING THE GOSPEL TO ALL MEN—AS WE ARE COMMANDED BY CHRIST TO DO—SO LONG AS THIS SIN IS NOT OVERCOME AND CAST OUT.

Many feel that the great need of missions is the obtaining of men and women who will give themselves to the Lord to strive in prayer for the salvation of souls. It has also been said that God is eager and able to deliver and bless the world he has redeemed, if his people were but willing, if they were but ready, to cry to him day and night. But how can congregations be brought to that unless there comes first an entire change in ministers and that they begin to see that the indispensable thing is not preaching, not pastoral visitation, not church work, but fellowship with God in prayer till they are clothed with power from on high?

Oh, that all thought and work and expectation concerning the kingdom might drive us to the acknowledgment of the sin of prayerlessness! God help us to root it out! God deliver us from it through the blood and power of Christ Jesus! God teach every minister of the Word to see what a glorious place he may occupy if he first of all is delivered from this root of evils; so that with courage and joy, in faith and perseverance, he can go on with his God!

The sin of prayerlessness! The Lord lay the burden of it so heavy on our hearts that we may not rest till it is taken far from us; through the name and power of Jesus He will make this possible for us....

THE CAUSE OF PRAYERLESSNESS.

In an elder's prayer meeting, a brother put the question: 'What, then, is the cause of so much prayerlessness? Is it not unbelief?'

The answer was: 'Certainly; but then comes the question what is the cause of that unbelief?' When the disciples asked the Lord Jesus: 'Why could not we cast the devil out?' His answer was: 'Because of your unbelief.' He went further and said: 'How beit this kind goeth not out but by prayer and fasting' (Matt. 17:19-21). If the life is not one of self-denial—of fasting—that is, letting the world go; of prayer—that is, laying hold of heaven, faith cannot be exercised. A life lived according to the flesh and not according to the Spirit—it is in this that we find the origin of the prayerlessness of which we complain. As we came out of the meeting a brother said to me: 'That is the whole difficulty; we wish to pray in the Spirit and at the same time walk after the flesh, and this is impossible.'

If one is sick and desires healing, it is of prime importance that the true cause of the sickness be discovered. This is always the first step toward recovery. If the particular cause is not recognized, and attention is directed to subordinate causes, or to supposed but not real causes, healing

4

is out of the question. In like manner, it is of the utmost importance for us to obtain a correct insight into the cause of the sad condition of deadness and failure in prayer in the inner chamber, which should be such a blessed place for us. Let us seek to realize fully what is the root of this evil.

Scripture teaches us that there are but two conditions possible for the Christian. One is a walk according to the Spirit, the other a walk according to 'the flesh'. These two powers are in irreconcilable conflict with each other. So it comes to pass, in the case of the majority of Christians, that, while we thank God that they are born again through the Spirit and have received the life of God—yet their ordinary daily life is not lived according to the Spirit but according to 'the flesh'. Paul writes to the Galatians: 'Are ye so foolish? Having begun in the Spirit, are ye now made perfect by the flesh?' (Gal. 3:3). Their service lay in fleshly outward performances. They did not understand that where 'the flesh' is permitted to influence their service of God, it soon results in open sin.

So he mentions not only grave sins as the work of 'the flesh', such as adultery, murder, drunkenness; but also the more ordinary sins of daily life—wrath, strife, variance; and he gives the exhortation: 'Walk in the Spirit, and ye shall not fulfill the lust of the flesh... If we live in the Spirit, let us also walk in the Spirit' (Gal. 5:16, 25). The Spirit must be honored not only as the author of a new life but also as the leader and director of our entire walk. Otherwise we are what the apostle calls 'carnal'.

The majority of Christians have little understanding of this matter. They have no real knowledge of the deep sinfulness and godlessness of that carnal nature which belongs to them and to which unconsciously they yield. 'God... condemned sin in the flesh' (Rom. 8:3) —in the cross of Christ. 'They that are Christ's have crucified the flesh with the affections and lusts' (Gal. 5:24). 'The flesh' cannot be improved or sanctified. 'The carnal mind is enmity against God; for it is not subject to the law of God, neither indeed can be' (Rom. 8:7). There is no means of dealing with 'the flesh' save as Christ dealt with it, bearing it to the cross. 'Our old man is crucified with him' (Rom. 6:6); so we by faith also crucify it, and regard and treat it daily as an accursed thing that finds its rightful place on the accursed cross.

It is saddening to consider how many Christians there are who seldom think or speak earnestly about the deep and immeasurable sinfulness of 'the flesh'— 'In me (that is, in my flesh) dwelleth no good thing' (Rom 7:18). The man who truly believes this may well cry out: 'I see another law in my members... bringing me into captivity to the law of sin... O wretched man that I am! Who shall deliver me from the body of this death?' (Rom. 7:23, 24). Happy is he who can go further and say: 'I thank God, through Jesus Christ our Lord... For the law of the Spirit of life in Christ Jesus hath made me free from the law of sin and death' (Rom. 7:25; 8:2).

Would that we might understand God's counsels of grace for us! 'The flesh' on the cross—the Spirit in the heart and controlling the life. This spiritual life is too little understood or sought after; yet it is literally what God has promised and will accomplish in those who unconditionally surrender themselves to him for this purpose.

Here then we have the deep root of evil as the cause of a prayerless life. 'The flesh' can say prayers well enough, calling itself religious for so doing and thus satisfying conscience. But 'the flesh' has no desire or strength for the prayer that strives after an intimate knowledge of God; that rejoices in fellowship with him; and that continues to lay hold of his strength. So, finally, it comes to this, 'the flesh' must be denied and crucified.

The Christian who is still carnal has neither disposition nor strength to follow after God. He rests satisfied with the prayer of habit or custom; but the glory, the blessedness of secret prayer is a hidden thing to him, till some day his eyes are opened, and he begins to see that 'the flesh', in its disposition to turn away from God, is the archenemy which makes powerful prayer impossible for him.

I had once, at a conference, spoken on the subject of prayer and made use of strong expressions about the enmity of 'the flesh' as a cause of prayerlessness. After the address, the minister's wife said that she thought I had spoken too strongly. She also had to mourn over too little desire for prayer, but she knew her heart was sincerely set on seeking God. I showed her what the word of God said about 'the flesh', and that everything which prevents the reception of the Spirit is nothing else than a secret work of 'the flesh'. Adam was created to have fellowship with God and enjoyed it before his fall. After the fall, however, there came immediately, a deep-seated aversion to God, and he fled from him. This incurable aversion is the characteristic of the unregenerate nature and the chief cause of our unwillingness to surrender ourselves to fellowship with God in prayer. The following day she told me that God had opened her eyes; she confessed that the enmity and unwillingness of 'the flesh' was the hidden hindrance in her defective prayer life.

O my brethren, do not seek to find in circumstances the explanation of this prayerlessness over which we mourn; seek it where God's word declares it to be, in the hidden aversion of the heart to a holy God.

When a Christian does not yield entirely to the leading of the Spirit—and this is certainly the will of God and the work of his grace—he lives, without knowing it, under the power of 'the flesh'. This life of 'the flesh' manifests itself in many different ways. It appears in the hastiness of spirit, or the anger which so unexpectedly arises in you, in the lack of love for which you have so often blamed yourself; in the pleasure found in eating and drinking, about which at times your conscience has chidden you; in that seeking for your own will and honor, that confidence in your own wisdom and power, that pleasure in the world, of which you are sometimes ashamed before God. All this is life 'after the flesh'. 'Ye are yet carnal' (1 Cor 3:3) that text, perhaps, disturbs you at times; you have not full peace and joy in God.

I pray you take time and give an answer to the question: Have I not found here the cause of my prayerlessness, of my powerlessness to effect any change in the matter? I live in the Spirit, I have been born again, but I do not walk after the Spirit—'the flesh' lords it over me. The carnal life cannot possibly pray in the spirit and power. God forgive me. The carnal life is evidently the cause of my sad and shameful prayerlessness.

Read this passage and underline all the phrases that describe the work of the Spirit.

In the first year of Darius the son of Ahasuerus, by descent a Mede, who was made king over the realm of the Chaldeans— **2** in the first year of his reign, I, Daniel, perceived in the books the number of years that, according to the word of the LORD to Jeremiah the prophet, must pass before the end of the desolations of Jerusalem, namely, seventy years.

3 Then I turned my face to the Lord God, seeking him by prayer and pleas for mercy with fasting and sackcloth and ashes. **4** I prayed to the LORD my God and made confession, saying, "O Lord, the great and awesome God, who keeps covenant and steadfast love with those who love him and keep his commandments, **5** we have sinned and done wrong and acted wickedly and rebelled, turning aside from your commandments and rules. **6** We have not listened to your servants the prophets, who spoke in your name to our kings, our princes, and our fathers, and to all the people of the land. **7** To you, O Lord, belongs righteousness, but to us open shame, as at this day, to the men of Judah, to the inhabitants of Jerusalem, and to all Israel, those who are near and those who are far away, in all the lands to which you have driven them, because of the treachery that they have committed against you. **8** To us, O LORD, belongs open shame, to our kings, to our princes, and to our fathers, because we have sinned against you. **9** To the Lord our God belong mercy and forgiveness, for we have rebelled against him **10** and have not obeyed the voice of the LORD our God by walking in his laws, which he set before us by his servants the prophets. **11** All Israel has transgressed your law and turned aside, refusing to obey your voice. And the curse and oath that are written in the Law of Moses the servant of God have been poured out upon us, because we have sinned against him. **12** He has confirmed his words, which he spoke against us and against our rulers who ruled us, by bringing upon us a great calamity. For under the whole heaven there has not been done anything like what has been done against Jerusalem. **13** As it is written in the Law of Moses, all this calamity has come upon us; yet we have not entreated the favor of the LORD our God, turning from our iniquities and gaining insight by your truth. **14** Therefore the LORD has kept ready the calamity and has brought it upon us, for the LORD our God is righteous in all the works that he has done, and we have not obeyed his voice. **15** And now, O Lord our God, who brought your people out of the land of Egypt with a mighty hand, and have made a name for yourself, as at this day, we have sinned, we have done wickedly.

16 "O Lord, according to all your righteous acts, let your anger and your wrath turn away from your city Jerusalem, your holy hill, because for our sins, and for the iniquities of our fathers, Jerusalem and your people have become a byword among all who are around us. **17** Now therefore, O our God, listen to the prayer of your servant and to his pleas for mercy, and for your own sake, O Lord, make your face to shine upon your sanctuary, which is desolate. **18** O my God, incline your ear and hear. Open your eyes and see our desolations, and the city that is called by your name. For we do not present our pleas before you because of our righteousness, but because of your great mercy. **19** O Lord, hear; O Lord, forgive. O Lord, pay attention and act. Delay not, for your own sake, O my God, because your city and your people are called by your name."

JOURNALING & MEDITATION

Consider the reasons behind the lack of prayer in your life? According to Murray, what lies at the heart of our prayerlessness? Would you agree with Murray? How does the sin of prayerlessness lead to so many other kinds of sin? *The flesh — self focus self interest*

CLOSING PRAYER

Take five to ten minutes to confess your sin of prayerlessness and the heart behind this sin.

DAY 2: THE FIGHT AGAINST PRAYERLESSNESS

As we looked yesterday at the sin of prayerlessness, we turn today to how we fight against that prayerlessness. In the midst of over-schedule, busy lives, making time to pray grows our ability to discern how the Spirit of God leads us to priorities we ought to have. Read this second excerpt from *The Believer's Prayer Life* by Andrew Murray.

. . .

The Fight Against Prayerlessness

As soon as the Christian becomes convinced of his sin in this matter, his first thought is that he must begin to strive, with God's help, to gain the victory over it. But alas, he soon experiences that his striving is worth little, and the discouraging thought comes over him, like a wave, that such a life is not for him—he cannot continue faithful! At conferences on the subject of prayer, held during the past years, many a minister has openly said that it seemed impossible for him to attain such a strict life.

Recently I received a letter from a minister, well known for his ability and devotion, in which he writes, 'As far as I am concerned, it does not seem to help me to hear too much about the life of prayer, about the strenuous exertion for which we must prepare ourselves, and about all the time and trouble and endless effort it will cost us. These things discourage me—I have so often heard them. I have time after time put them to the test, and the result has always been sadly disappointing.
It does not help me to be told: 'You must pray more, and hold a closer watch over yourself, and become altogether a more earnest Christian.'

My reply to him was as follows: 'I think in all I spoke at the conference or elsewhere, I have never mentioned exertion or struggle, because I am so entirely convinced that our efforts are futile unless we first learn how to abide in Christ by a simple faith.'

My correspondent said further: 'The message I need is this: "See that your relationship to your living Savior is what it ought to be. Live in his presence, rejoice in his love, rest in him."' A better message could not be given, if it is only rightly understood. 'See that your relationship to the living Savior is what it ought to be.' But this is just what will certainly make it possible for one to live the life of prayer.

We must not comfort ourselves with the thought of standing in a right relationship to the Lord Jesus while the sin of prayerlessness has power over us, and while we, along with the whole Church, have to complain about our feeble life which makes us unfit to pray for ourselves, for the Church, or for missions, as we ought. But if we recognize, in the first place, that a right relationship to the Lord Jesus, above all else, includes prayer, with both the desire and power to pray according to God's will, then we have something which gives us the right to rejoice in him and to rest in him.

I have related this incident to point out how naturally discouragement will be the result of self-effort and will so shut out all hope of improvement or victory. And this indeed is the condition of many Christians when called on to persevere in prayer as intercessors. They feel it is certainly something entirely beyond their reach—they have not the power for the self-sacrifice and consecration necessary for such prayer; they shrink from the effort and struggle which will, as they suppose, make them unhappy. They have tried in the power of the flesh to conquer the flesh—a wholly impossible thing... It is Jesus alone who can subdue the flesh and the devil.

We have spoken of a struggle which will certainly result in disappointment and discouragement. This is the effort made in our own strength. But there is another struggle which will certainly lead to victory.

The Scripture speaks of 'the good fight of faith', that is to say, a fight which springs from and is carried on by faith. We must get right conceptions about faith and stand fast in our faith. Jesus Christ is ever the author and finisher of faith. It is when we come into right relationship with him that we can be sure of the help and power he bestows. Just, then, as earnestly as we must, in the first place, say: 'Do not strive in your own strength; cast yourself at the feet of the Lord Jesus, and wait upon him in the sure confidence that he is with you, and works in you'; so do we, in the second place, say: 'Strive in prayer; let faith fill your heart—so will you be strong in the Lord, and in the power of his might.'

An illustration will help us to understand this. A devoted Christian woman who conducted a large Bible class with zeal and success once came in trouble to her minister. In her earlier years she had enjoyed much blessing in the inner chamber, in fellowship with the Lord and his word. But this had gradually been lost and, do what she would, she could not get right. The Lord had blessed her work, but the joy had gone out of her life. The minister asked what she had done to regain the lost blessedness. 'I have done everything,' said she, 'that I can think of, but all in vain.'

He then questioned her about her experience in connection with her conversion. She gave an immediate and clear answer: 'At first I spared no pains in my attempt to become better, and to free myself from sin, but it was all useless. At last I began to understand that I must lay aside all my efforts, and simply trust the Lord Jesus to bestow on me his life and peace, and he did it.'

'Why then,' said the minister, 'do you not try this again? As you go to your inner chamber, however cold and dark your heart may be, do not try in your own might to force yourself into the right attitude. Bow before him, and tell him that he sees in what a sad state you are that your only hope is in him. Trust him with a childlike trust to have mercy upon you, and wait upon him. In such a trust you are in a right relationship to him. You have nothing; he has everything.' Some time later she told the minister that his advice had helped her; she had learned that faith in the love of the Lord Jesus is the only method of getting into fellowship with God in prayer.

Do you not begin to see, my reader, that there are two kinds of warfare—the first when we seek to conquer prayerlessness in our own strength? In that case, my advice to you is: 'Give over your restlessness and effort; fall helpless at the feet of the Lord Jesus; he will speak the word, and your soul will live.' If you have done this, then, second, comes the message: 'This is but the beginning of everything. It will require deep earnestness, and the exercise of all your power, and a watchfulness of the entire heart—eager to detect the least backsliding. Above all, it will require a surrender to a life of self-sacrifice that God really desires to see in us and which he will work out for us.'

Read this passage and consider the main point of what Jesus was trying to teach his disciples through this passage.

"I am the true vine, and my Father is the vinedresser. **2** Every branch in me that does not bear fruit he takes away, and every branch that does bear fruit he prunes, that it may bear more fruit. **3** Already you are clean because of the word that I have spoken to you. Abide in me, and I in you. As the branch cannot bear fruit by itself, unless it abides in the vine, neither can you, unless you abide in me. **5** I am the vine; you are the branches. Whoever abides in me and I in him, he it is that bears much fruit, for apart from me you can do nothing. **6** If anyone does not abide in me he is thrown away like a branch and withers; and the branches are gathered, thrown into the fire, and burned. **7** If you abide in me, and my words abide in you, ask whatever you wish, and it will be done for you. **8** By this my Father is glorified, that you bear much fruit and so prove to be my disciples. **9** As the Father has loved me, so have I loved you. Abide in my love. **10** If you keep my commandments, you will abide in my love, just as I have kept my Father's commandments and abide in his love. **11** These things I have spoken to you, that my joy may be in you, and that your joy may be full.

12 "This is my commandment, that you love one another as I have loved you. **13** Greater love has no one than this, that someone lay down his life for his friends. **14** You are my friends if you do what I command you. **15** No longer do I call you servants, for the servant does not know what his master is doing; but I have called you friends, for all that I have heard from my Father I have made known to you. **16** You did not choose me, but I chose you and appointed you that you should go and bear fruit and that your fruit should abide, so that whatever you ask the Father in my name, he may give it to you. **17** These things I command you, so that you will love one another.

...

26 "But when the Helper comes, whom I will send to you from the Father, the Spirit of truth, who proceeds from the Father, he will bear witness about me.

"I have said all these things to you to keep you from falling away. [2] They will put you out of the synagogues. Indeed, the hour is coming when whoever kills you will think he is offering service to God. [3] And they will do these things because they have not known the Father, nor me. [4] But I have said these things to you, that when their hour comes you may remember that I told them to you.

"I did not say these things to you from the beginning, because I was with you. [5] But now I am going to him who sent me, and none of you asks me, 'Where are you going?' [6] But because I have said these things to you, sorrow has filled your heart. [7] Nevertheless, I tell you the truth: it is to your advantage that I go away, for if I do not go away, the Helper will not come to you. But if I go, I will send him to you. [8] And when he comes, he will convict the world concerning sin and righteousness and judgment: [9] concerning sin, because they do not believe in me; [10] concerning righteousness, because I go to the Father, and you will see me no longer; [11] concerning judgment, because the ruler of this world is judged.

[12] "I still have many things to say to you, but you cannot bear them now. [13] When the Spirit of truth comes, he will guide you into all the truth, for he will not speak on his own authority, but whatever he hears he will speak, and he will declare to you the things that are to come. [14] He will glorify me, for he will take what is mine and declare it to you. [15] All that the Father has is mine; therefore I said that he will take what is mine and declare it to you.

SUMMARIZE

One significant point that stood out to you in this passage.

Abide If you abide in Me and My
Words abide in you,
ask whatever you wish,
and it will be done for you.

JOURNALING & MEDITATION

When we want to get something done, we often think it's a matter of discipline and scheduling; however, prayer is much more than this. Murray's chapter and this Biblical passage remind us how dependent we are on Christ for all growth in the Christian life. What does "abiding in Christ" look like in your life?

PRAYER

Take time to consider and confess your self reliant and self-sufficient tendencies. How is this manifesting in your life right now? Admit to Christ your utter dependence on Him and allow His Spirit to strengthen you.

DAY 3: INTRODUCTION

Psalm 27

1 The LORD is my light and my salvation; whom shall I fear?
   The LORD is the stronghold of my life; of whom shall I be afraid?
2 When evildoers assail me to eat up my flesh,
   my adversaries and foes, it is they who stumble and fall.
3 Though an army encamp against me, my heart shall not fear;
   though war arise against me, yet I will be confident.
4 One thing have I asked of the LORD, that will I seek after:
   that I may dwell in the house of the LORD all the days of my life,
   to gaze upon the beauty of the LORD and to inquire in his temple.
5 For he will hide me in his shelter in the day of trouble;
   he will conceal me under the cover of his tent;
he will lift me high upon a rock.
6 And now my head shall be lifted up above my enemies all around
me,
   and I will offer in his tent sacrifices with shouts of joy;
   I will sing and make melody to the LORD.
7 Hear, O LORD, when I cry aloud; be gracious to me and answer
me!
8 You have said, "Seek my face."
   My heart says to you, "Your face, LORD, do I seek."
9 Hide not your face from me.
   Turn not your servant away in anger, O you who have been my
help.
   Cast me not off; forsake me not, O God of my salvation!
10 For my father and my mother have forsaken me,
but the LORD will take me in.
11 Teach me your way, O LORD,
and lead me on a level path because of my enemies.
12 Give me not up to the will of my adversaries;
for false witnesses have risen against me, and they breathe out
violence.

13 *I believe that I shall look upon the goodness of the* LORD
in the land of the living!
14 *Wait for the* LORD*; be strong, and let your heart take courage;*
wait for the LORD*!*

PREPARATION

Today we turn to the Lord's Prayer and begin with an overview of this most famous of Christian prayers. Read the follow excerpt from *Praying the Lord's Prayer* by J.I. Packer.

◆ ◆ ◆

"It is not too much to say that God made us to pray, that prayer is (not the easiest, but) the most natural activity in which we ever engage, and that prayer is the measure of us all in God's sight. "What a man is alone on his knees before God," said the saintly Murray McCheyne, "that he is—and no more." Perhaps Jesus' disciples felt this when they made their momentous request (have you ever echoed it?), "Lord, teach us to pray" (Luke 11:1). Jesus must have rejoiced to be asked this. In the manner of a good teacher, however, he controlled his feelings and gave a matter-of-fact answer. "When you pray, say..." and for the second time in his public ministry he gave them the form of words that we call the Lord's Prayer (Luke 11:2-4; cf. Matthew 6:9-13).

"Say..." Did Jesus just intend that they should repeat the words, parrot fashion? No; but that they should enter into the sense. "Say," we might say, means "mean!" This prayer is a pattern for all Christian praying. Jesus is teaching that prayer will be acceptable when, and only when, the attitudes, thoughts, and desires expressed fit the pattern. That is to say: every prayer of ours should be a praying of the Lord's Prayer in some shape or form."

*Now Jesus was praying in a certain place, and when he finished, one of his disciples said to him, "Lord, teach us to pray, as John taught his disciples." **2** And he said to them, "When you pray, say:*

"Father, hallowed be your name.

Your kingdom come.

3 *Give us each day our daily bread,*

4 *and forgive us our sins,*

for we ourselves forgive everyone who is indebted to us.

And lead us not into temptation."

5 *And he said to them, "Which of you who has a friend will go to him at midnight and say to him, 'Friend, lend me three loaves, **6** for a friend of mine has arrived on a journey, and I have nothing to set before him'; **7** and he will answer from within, 'Do not bother me; the door is now shut, and my children are with me in bed. I cannot get up and give you anything'? **8** I tell you, though he will not get up and give him anything because he is his friend, yet because of his impudence he will rise and give him whatever he needs. **9** And I tell you, ask, and it will be given to you; seek, and you will find; knock, and it will be opened to you. **10** For everyone who asks receives, and the one who seeks finds, and to the one who knocks it will be opened. **11** What father among you, if his son asks for a fish, will instead of a fish give him a serpent; **12** or if he asks for an egg, will give him a scorpion? **13** If you then, who are evil, know how to give good gifts to your children, how much more will the heavenly Father give the Holy Spirit to those who ask him!" "*

JOURNALING & MEDITATION

Consider the prayers that you first prayed when you became a Christian. How have your prayers changed over the years? In what ways has your prayer life matured and in what ways has it gotten worse? As we think about where we should be in our prayer lives, it's safe to say that, like the disciples, we need to approach Jesus and ask him "to teach us to pray". How would you like to grow in your prayer life?

PRAYER

Take some time to ask God to speak to you through the course of this devotional and lead you to a deeper understanding and experience of prayer.

DAY 4: THE LORD'S PRAYER

OPENING MEDITATION

Psalm 139

1   *O LORD, you have searched me and known me!*

2   *You know when I sit down and when I rise up;*
       you discern my thoughts from afar.

3   *You search out my path and my lying down*
       and are acquainted with all my ways.

4   *Even before a word is on my tongue,*
       behold, O LORD, you know it altogether.

5   *You hem me in, behind and before,*
       and lay your hand upon me.

6   *Such knowledge is too wonderful for me;*
       it is high; I cannot attain it.

7   *Where shall I go from your Spirit?*
       Or where shall I flee from your presence?

8   *If I ascend to heaven, you are there!*
       If I make my bed in Sheol, you are there!

9   *If I take the wings of the morning*
       and dwell in the uttermost parts of the sea,

10   *even there your hand shall lead me,*
       and your right hand shall hold me.

11   *If I say, "Surely the darkness shall cover me,*
       and the light about me be night,"

12   *even the darkness is not dark to you;*
       the night is bright as the day,
       for darkness is as light with you.

13   *For you formed my inward parts;*
       you knitted me together in my mother's womb.

14   *I praise you, for I am fearfully and wonderfully made.*
       Wonderful are your works;
       my soul knows it very well.

15   *My frame was not hidden from you,*
       when I was being made in secret,
       intricately woven in the depths of the earth.

16   *Your eyes saw my unformed substance;*

in your book were written, every one of them,
the days that were formed for me,
when as yet there was none of them.
17   How precious to me are your thoughts, O God!
How vast is the sum of them!
18   If I would count them, they are more than the sand.
I awake, and I am still with you.
19   Oh that you would slay the wicked, O God!
O men of blood, depart from me!
20   They speak against you with malicious intent;
your enemies take your name in vain.
21   Do I not hate those who hate you, O LORD?
And do I not loathe those who rise up against you?
22   I hate them with complete hatred;
I count them my enemies.
23   Search me, O God, and know my heart!
Try me and know my thoughts!
24   And see if there be any grievous way in me,
and lead me in the way everlasting!

PREPARATION

The following excerpt from Packer helps us understand the rich diversity of this prayer and how it encourages us broaden our interactions with God.

"As analysis of light requires reference to the seven colors of the spectrum that make it up, so analysis of the Lord's Prayer requires reference to a spectrum of seven distinct activities: *approaching* God in adoration and trust; *acknowledging* his work and his worth, in praise and worship; *admitting* sin, and seeking pardon; *asking* that needs be met, for ourselves and others; *arguing* with God for blessing, as wrestling Jacob did in Genesis 32 (God loves to be argued with); *accepting* from God one's own situation as he has shaped it; and adhering to God in faithfulness through thick and thin. These seven activities together constitute biblical prayer, and the Lord's Prayer embodies them all. "

—J. I. Packer, *Praying the Lord's Prayer*

5 *"And when you pray, you must not be like the hypocrites. For they love to stand and pray in the synagogues and at the street corners, that they may be seen by others. Truly, I say to you, they have received their reward.* **6** *But when you pray, go into your room and shut the door and pray to* <u>your Father who is in secret</u>. *And* <u>your Father who sees in secret</u> *will reward you.*

7 *"And when you pray, do not heap up empty phrases as the Gentiles do, for they think that they will be heard for their many words.* **8** *Do not be like them, for your Father knows what you need before you ask him.* **9** *Pray then like this:*

"Our Father in heaven, hallowed be your name.
10 *Your kingdom come,*
your will be done, on earth as it is in heaven.
11 *Give us this day our daily bread,*
12 *and forgive us our debts,*
as we also have forgiven our debtors.
13 *And lead us not into temptation,*
but deliver us from evil.

14 *For if you forgive others their trespasses, your heavenly Father will also forgive you,* **15** *but if you do not forgive others their trespasses, neither will your Father forgive your trespasses.*

SUMMARIZE

One key point that stood out to you in this passage.

Secret – private, personal

JOURNALING & MEDITATION

Take time to read through the seven divisions of the Lord's prayer found in the Preparation section. When you typically pray, which section do you focus upon and which sections do you tend to neglect? Write your own paraphrase of the Lord's Prayer incorporating each of these sections.

- arguing
- accepting = adhering

PRAYER

Internalize your paraphrased prayer as you commune with the Lord. As you pray, be reminded of God's presence and His desire to have fellowship with you.

DAY 5: OUR FATHER

Intimacy and Revolution

We begin today focusing upon those first words of the Lord's Prayer—"Our Father". The Scriptures provide a rich context for this phrase and the following passage from N.T. Wright will provide some helpful background before we look at some passages in Scripture that help us understand the Fatherhood of God.

> "People used to say that nobody before Jesus had called God 'Father'. They also used to say that the word 'Abba,' which Jesus used in the Garden of Gethsemane and quite possibly on other occasions, was the little child's word, 'Daddy', in the Hebrew or Aramaic of his day. People therefore used to say that Jesus thus introduced, and offered to the world, a new level of personal intimacy with God. This conclusion may, in some sense, be true; but the two pillars on which it stood are shaky. Plenty of people called God 'Father', in Judaism and elsewhere. And Abba is in fact a word with much wider use than simply on the lips of little children. So what did it mean for Jesus himself that he called God 'Father'?
>
> The most important thing, which is really the starting-point for grasping who Jesus was and is, is that this word drew into one point the vocation of Israel, and particularly the salvation of Israel. The first occurrence in the Hebrew Bible of the idea of God as the Father comes when Moses marches in boldly to stand before Pharaoh, and says; Thus says YHWH: Israel is my son, my firstborn; let my people go, that they may serve me (Exodus 4:22-3). For Israel to call God 'Father', then, was to hold on to the hope of liberty. The slaves were called to be sons.
>
> When Jesus tells his disciples to call God 'Father', then, those with ears to hear will understand. He wants us to get ready for the new Exodus. We are going to be free at last. This is the Advent hope, the hope of the coming of the Kingdom of God. The tyrant's grip is going to be broken, and we shall be free: I see my light come shining, From the west down to the east. Any

24

day now - any day now - I shall be released. The very first word of the Lord's Prayer, therefore (in Greek or Aramaic, 'Father' would come first), contains within it not just intimacy, but revolution. Not just familiarity; hope."

—N. T. Wright, *The Lord and His Prayer*

TEXT: HOSEA 11:1-11 | THE LORD'S LOVE FOR ISRAEL

Read this text slowly and meditatively three times. Between each reading, sit still in silence for 2 minutes and allow God's Spirit to communicate to you who He is. On your third reading, personalize this text and allow God to speak to you in the here and now.

1   *When Israel was a child, I loved him,*
      and out of Egypt I called my son.

2   *The more they were called, the more they went away;*
   they kept sacrificing to the Baals
   and burning offerings to idols.

3   *Yet it was I who taught Ephraim to walk;*
   I took them up by their arms,
   but they did not know that I healed them.

4   *I led them with cords of kindness, with the bands of love,*
   and I became to them as one who eases the yoke on their jaws, and I bent down to them and fed them.

5   *They shall not return to the land of Egypt,*
   but Assyria shall be their king,
   because they have refused to return to me.

6   *The sword shall rage against their cities,*
   consume the bars of their gates,
   and devour them because of their own counsels.

7   *My people are bent on turning away from me,*
   and though they call out to the Most High,
   he shall not raise them up at all.

8   *How can I give you up, O Ephraim?*
   How can I hand you over, O Israel?
   How can I make you like Admah?
   How can I treat you like Zeboiim?
   My heart recoils within me;
   my compassion grows warm and tender.

9   *I will not execute my burning anger;*

> *I will not again destroy Ephraim;*
> *for I am God and not a man,*
> *the Holy One in your midst, and I will not come in wrath.*
> 10 *They shall go after the LORD;*
> *he will roar like a lion; when he roars,*
> *his children shall come trembling from the west;*
> 11 *they shall come trembling like birds from Egypt,*
> *and like doves from the land of Assyria,*
> *and I will return them to their homes, declares the LORD.*

SUMMARIZE

How does this passage reflect both intimacy and revolution?

JOURNALING & MEDITATION

As Wright points out, when we call God "Father" it is a term of both affection and revolution. God as our Father has done something utterly remarkable. He has not only adopted us as his children but as children he has brought us into the larger narrative of his cosmic redemption. Take time to write down who God is as a Father who is both intimately near and sovereignly transcendent over all the world. How can you love and adore God for both of these aspects of his character?

Based on today's Bible passages and reflection, spend 10 minutes in prayer focusing solely on this phrase "Our Father".

DAY 6: OUR FATHER

Adoption

The Lord's Prayer does not begin with us, but begins with God and God as Father. It reminds us that our lives do not center around ourselves, but that our lives can only be properly understood when we know who God is as our Father. Calling God "Father" brings to us an incredible sense of who we are, re-anchoring us in the privilege of being his adopted children. Read the following excerpt to remind you of the significance of being His child.

> "Justification is the basic blessing, on which adoption is founded; adoption is the crowning blessing, to which justification clears the way. Adopted status belongs to all who receive Christ (John 1:12). The adopted status of believers means that in and through Christ God loves them as he loves his only-begotten Son and will share with them all the glory that is Christ's now (Rom. 8:17, 38-39). Here and now, believers are under God's fatherly care and discipline (Matt. 6:26; Heb. 12:5-11) and are directed, especially by Jesus, to live their whole lives in light of the knowledge that God is their Father in heaven. They are to pray to him as such (Matt. 6:5-13), imitate him as such (Matt. 5:44-48; 6:12, 14-15; 18:21-35; Eph. 4:32–5:2), and trust him as such (Matt. 6:25-34), thus expressing the filial instinct that the Holy Spirit has implanted in them (Rom. 8:15-17; Gal. 4:6). Adoption and regeneration accompany each other as two aspects of the salvation that Christ brings (John 1:12-13), but they are to be distinguished. Adoption is the bestowal of a relationship, while regeneration is the transformation of our moral nature. Yet the link is evident; God wants his children, whom he loves, to bear his character, and takes action accordingly."

> *- J. I. Packer, Concise Theology : A Guide to Historic Christian Beliefs*

When we lose sight of this inestimable privilege we have received in adoption, our lives can be characterized by a prodigal chasing after what we already have because of Christ. Read the following passages and consider who we are in light of God as our Father.

11 And he said, "There was a man who had two sons. 12 And the younger of them said to his father, 'Father, give me the share of property that is coming to me.' And he divided his property between them. 13 Not many days later, the younger son gathered all he had and took a journey into a far country, and there he squandered his property in reckless living. 14 And when he had spent everything, a severe famine arose in that country, and he began to be in need. 15 So he went and hired himself out to one of the citizens of that country, who sent him into his fields to feed pigs. 16 And he was longing to be fed with the pods that the pigs ate, and no one gave him anything.

17 "But when he came to himself, he said, 'How many of my father's hired servants have more than enough bread, but I perish here with hunger! 18 I will arise and go to my father, and I will say to him, "Father, I have sinned against heaven and before you. 19 I am no longer worthy to be called your son. Treat me as one of your hired servants." ' 20 And he arose and came to his father. But while he was still a long way off, his father saw him and felt compassion, and ran and embraced him and kissed him. 21 And the son said to him, 'Father, I have sinned against heaven and before you. I am no longer worthy to be called your son.' 22 But the father said to his servants, 'Bring quickly the best robe, and put it on him, and put a ring on his hand, and shoes on his feet. 23 And bring the fattened calf and kill it, and let us eat and celebrate. 24 For this my son was dead, and is alive again; he was lost, and is found.' And they began to celebrate.

25 "Now his older son was in the field, and as he came and drew near to the house, he heard music and dancing. 26 And he called one of the servants and asked what these things meant. 27 And he said to him, 'Your brother has come, and your father has killed the fattened calf, because he has received him back safe and sound.' 28 But he was angry and refused to go in. His father came out and entreated him, 29 but he answered his father, 'Look, these many years I have served you, and I never disobeyed your command, yet you never gave me a young goat, that I might celebrate with my friends. 30 But when this son of yours came, who has devoured your property with prostitutes, you killed the fattened calf for him!' 31 And he said to him, 'Son, you are always with me, and all that is mine is yours. **32** *It was fitting to celebrate and be glad, for this your brother was dead, and is alive; he was lost, and is found.' "*

TEXT: ROMANS 8:1-17 | LIFE IN THE SPIRIT

As you read this text underline all the benefits you have received being God's child.

There is therefore now no condemnation for those who are in Christ Jesus. **2** *For the law of the Spirit of life has set you free in Christ Jesus from the law of sin and death.* **3** *For God has done what the law, weakened by the flesh, could not do. By sending his own Son in the likeness of sinful flesh and for sin, he condemned sin in the flesh,* **4** *in order that the righteous requirement of the law might be fulfilled in us, who walk not according to the flesh but according to the Spirit.* **5** *For those who live according to the flesh set their minds on the things of the flesh, but those who live according to the Spirit set their minds on the things of the Spirit.* **6** *For to set the mind on the flesh is death, but to set the mind on the Spirit is life and peace.* **7** *For the mind that is set on the flesh is hostile to God, for it does not submit to God's law; indeed, it cannot.* **8** *Those who are in the flesh cannot please God.*

9 *You, however, are not in the flesh but in the Spirit, if in fact the Spirit of God dwells in you. Anyone who does not have the Spirit of Christ does not belong to him.* **10** *But if Christ is in you, although the body is dead because of sin, the Spirit is life because of righteousness.* **11** *If the Spirit of him who raised Jesus from the dead dwells in you, he who raised Christ Jesus from the dead will also give life to your mortal bodies through his Spirit who dwells in you.*

12 *So then, brothers, we are debtors, not to the flesh, to live according to the flesh.* **13** *For if you live according to the flesh you will die, but if by the Spirit you put to death the deeds of the body, you will live.* **14** *For all who are led by the Spirit of God are sons of God.* **15** *For you did not receive the spirit of slavery to fall back into fear, but you have received the Spirit of adoption as sons, by whom we cry, "Abba! Father!"* **16** *The Spirit himself bears witness with our spirit that we are children of God,* **17** *and if children, then heirs—heirs of God and fellow heirs with Christ, provided we suffer with him in order that we may also be glorified with him.*

When we remember whose we are, the doubt and fear that often linger in our hearts are quickly displaced by joy and freedom. Consider this entry from the Welsh Methodist Revivalist.

> "On June 18, 1735, being in secret prayer, I felt suddenly my heart melting within me like wax before the fire with love to God my Savior. I felt not only love and peace, but also a longing to be dissolved and to be with Christ, and there was a cry in my inmost soul with which I was totally unacquainted before. It was this— 'Abba, Father; Abba, Father.' I could not help calling God my Father: I knew that I was His child, and that He loved me; my soul being filled and satiated, cried, 'It is enough—I am satisfied; give me strength, and I will follow Thee through fire and water.' I could now say that I was happy indeed. There was in me a well of water, springing up into everlasting life; yea, the love of God was shed abroad in my heart by the Holy Ghost."
>
> — *Howell Harris (1735)*

How have you lost sight of your identity as God's child? When we forget our identity as a child we revert to being a slave to something else. In what areas of your life do you still live as a slave? How is this leading to a "prodigal" lifestyle?

What would it look like if you actually believed some of the truths you underlined in Romans 8? What concerns would this address in your life? Take time to allow these truths to penetrate and soak into the doubts that you have.

PRAYER

Based on today's Bible passages and reflection on adoption, spend 10 minutes in prayer focusing solely on this phrase "Our Father".

DAY 7: IN HEAVEN

A Heavenly Father

Today we focus on one more characteristic of our Father and that is his being "in heaven". Consider the following description of heaven given by Packer:

> "Since God is spirit, 'heaven' here cannot signify a place remote from us that he inhabits. The Greek gods were thought of as spending most of their time far away from earth in the celestial equivalent of the Bahamas, but the God of the Bible is not like this. Granted, the 'heaven' where saints and angels dwell has to be thought of as a sort of locality, because saints and angels, as God's creatures, exist in space and time; but when the Creator is said to be 'in heaven,' the thought is that he exists on a different plane from us, rather than in a different place. That God in heaven is always near to his children on earth is something that the Bible takes for granted throughout.

> Because God is in Heaven, there is no place where He cannot be or cannot see. God's being in Heaven doesn't communicate that He is far from us, but rather the very opposite—that He is near. He is a holy God who is near to His children. There is not a place on this earth where our cries will not be heard by our Father."

> — *J. I. Packer. Praying the Lord's Prayer*

Psalm 91

1   *He who dwells in the shelter of the Most High*
will abide in the shadow of the Almighty.
2   *I will say to the* LORD, *"My refuge and my fortress,*
my God, in whom I trust."
3   *For he will deliver you from the snare of the fowler*
and from the deadly pestilence.
4   *He will cover you with his pinions,*
and under his wings you will find refuge;
his faithfulness is a shield and buckler.
5   *You will not fear the terror of the night,*
nor the arrow that flies by day,
6   *nor the pestilence that stalks in darkness,*
nor the destruction that wastes at noonday.
7   *A thousand may fall at your side,*
ten thousand at your right hand, but it will not come near you.
8   *You will only look with your eyes*
and see the recompense of the wicked.
9   *Because you have made the* LORD *your dwelling place—*
the Most High, who is my refuge—
10   *no evil shall be allowed to befall you,*
no plague come near your tent.
11   *For he will command his angels concerning you*
to guard you in all your ways.
12   *On their hands they will bear you up,*
lest you strike your foot against a stone.
13   *You will tread on the lion and the adder;*
the young lion and the serpent you will trample underfoot.
14   *"Because he holds fast to me in love, I will deliver him;*
I will protect him, because he knows my name.
15   *When he calls to me, I will answer him;*
I will be with him in trouble;
I will rescue him and honor him.
16   *With long life I will satisfy him and show him my*
salvation."

TEXT: ISAIAH 40: 9-26 | THE GREATNESS OF GOD

Underline all the phrases that communicate God's involvement in this world.

9 *Go on up to a high mountain, O Zion, herald of good news;*
lift up your voice with strength,
O Jerusalem, herald of good news;
lift it up, fear not;
say to the cities of Judah,
 "Behold your God!"

10 *Behold, the Lord GOD comes with might, and his arm rules*
for him;
 behold, his reward is with him, and his recompense before
him.

11 *He will tend his flock like a shepherd;*
he will gather the lambs in his arms;
 he will carry them in his bosom,
and gently lead those that are with young.

12 *Who has measured the waters in the hollow of his hand*
and marked off the heavens with a span,
 enclosed the dust of the earth in a measure
and weighed the mountains in scales and the hills in a balance?

13 *Who has measured the Spirit of the LORD,*
or what man shows him his counsel?

14 *Whom did he consult,*
and who made him understand?
 Who taught him the path of justice,
and taught him knowledge,
and showed him the way of understanding?

15 *Behold, the nations are like a drop from a bucket,*
and are accounted as the dust on the scales;
behold, he takes up the coastlands like fine dust.

16 *Lebanon would not suffice for fuel,*
nor are its beasts enough for a burnt offering.

17 *All the nations are as nothing before him,*
they are accounted by him as less than nothing and emptiness.

18 *To whom then will you liken God,*
or what likeness compare with him?

¹⁹ An idol! A craftsman casts it,
and a goldsmith overlays it with gold
and casts for it silver chains.
²⁰ He who is too impoverished for an offering
chooses wood that will not rot;
he seeks out a skillful craftsman
to set up an idol that will not move.
²¹ Do you not know? Do you not hear?
Has it not been told you from the beginning?
Have you not understood from the foundations of the earth?
²² It is he who sits above the circle of the earth,
and its inhabitants are like grasshoppers;
who stretches out the heavens like a curtain,
and spreads them like a tent to dwell in;
²³ who brings princes to nothing,
and makes the rulers of the earth as emptiness.
²⁴ Scarcely are they planted, scarcely sown,
scarcely has their stem taken root in the earth,
when he blows on them, and they wither,
and the tempest carries them off like stubble.
²⁵ To whom then will you compare me,
that I should be like him? says the Holy One.
²⁶ Lift up your eyes on high and see: who created these?
He who brings out their host by number, calling them all by name,
by the greatness of his might,
and because he is strong in power not one is missing.

SUMMARIZE

What stands out to you concerning the nature of God from the
previous passage.

JOURNALING & MEDITATION

In our day-to-day lives, we often think of God as being "out there" in heaven as if it were past Pluto and occasionally God comes down to "check in" on his people. However, the Biblical conception of heaven is quite different. It communicates an active involvement in the affairs of this world. Our God who is in heaven is a God who is magnificently near to us. What difference does it make to think that God sees all that we do and hears all that we say including all our pleas, cries, slander, and gossip? If you really believed this, how would it impact your prayer life?

PRAYER

Based on today's Bible passages and reflection, spend 10 minutes in prayer focusing solely on this phrase "In Heaven".

DAY 8: HALLOWED BE THY NAME

Hallowing God's Name

Hallowing God's name means to acknowledge, ascribe, and honor God as holy, and so when we pray this petition we join the heavenly hosts who proclaim that God is holy, holy, holy. Packer describes God's holiness in the following way:

> "When Scripture calls God, or individual persons of the Godhead, 'holy' (as it often does: Lev. 11:44-45; Josh. 24:19; Isa. 2:2; Ps. 99:9; Isa. 1:4; 6:3; 41:14, 16, 20; 57:15; Ezek. 39:7; Amos 4:2; John 17:11; Acts 5:3-4, 32; Rev. 15:4), the word signifies everything about God that sets him apart from us and makes him an object of awe, adoration, and dread to us. It covers all aspects of his transcendent greatness and moral perfection and thus is an attribute, of all his attributes, pointing to the 'Godness' of God at every point. Every facet of God's nature and every aspect of his character may properly be spoken of as holy, just because it is his. The core of the concept, however, is God's purity, which cannot tolerate any form of sin (Hab. 1:13) and thus calls sinners to constant self-abasement in his presence (Isa. 6:5)."

> — *J. I. Packer, Concise Theology : A Guide to Historic Christian Beliefs*

In the course of our day-to-day lives, we lose sight of God's holiness. We don't stand in awe of who He is. We are awed by many other things in the world, without realizing those things are just faint shadows compared to God's overwhelming brilliance. As we ascribe to God the holiness due His name, it realigns our lives to who is ultimately deserving of all fear, praise, wonder, awe, loyalty, adoration and unswerving devotion.

Revelation 4

After this I looked, and behold, a door standing open in heaven! And the first voice, which I had heard speaking to me like a trumpet, said, "Come up here, and I will show you what must take place after this." 2 At once I was in the Spirit, and behold, a throne stood in heaven, with one seated on the throne. 3 And he who sat there had the appearance of jasper and carnelian, and around the throne was a rainbow that had the appearance of an emerald. 4 Around the throne were twenty-four thrones, and seated on the thrones were twenty-four elders, clothed in white garments, with golden crowns on their heads. 5 From the throne came flashes of lightning, and rumblings and peals of thunder, and before the throne were burning seven torches of fire, which are the seven spirits of God, 6 and before the throne there was as it were a sea of glass, like crystal.

And around the throne, on each side of the throne, are four living creatures, full of eyes in front and behind: 7 the first living creature like a lion, the second living creature like an ox, the third living creature with the face of a man, and the fourth living creature like an eagle in flight. 8 And the four living creatures, each of them with six wings, are full of eyes all around and within, and day and night they never cease to say,

> *"Holy, holy, holy, is the Lord God Almighty,*
> *who was and is and is to come!"*

9 And whenever the living creatures give glory and honor and thanks to him who is seated on the throne, who lives forever and ever, 10 the twenty-four elders fall down before him who is seated on the throne and worship him who lives forever and ever. They cast their crowns before the throne, saying,

> 11   *"Worthy are you, our Lord and God,*
> *to receive glory and honor and power,*
> *for you created all things,*
> *and by your will they existed and were created."*

Read the following text from the book of Job where God answers Job in the midst of his misery.

Then the LORD answered Job out of the whirlwind and said:

2 "Who is this that darkens counsel by words without knowledge?

3 Dress for action like a man;
I will question you, and you make it known to me.

4 "Where were you when I laid the foundation of the earth?
Tell me, if you have understanding.

5 Who determined its measurements—surely you know!
Or who stretched the line upon it?

6 On what were its bases sunk,
or who laid its cornerstone,

7 when the morning stars sang together
and all the sons of God shouted for joy?

8 "Or who shut in the sea with doors
when it burst out from the womb,

9 when I made clouds its garment
and thick darkness its swaddling band,

10 and prescribed limits for it
and set bars and doors,

11 and said, 'Thus far shall you come, and no farther,
and here shall your proud waves be stayed'?

12 "Have you commanded the morning since your days began,
and caused the dawn to know its place,

13 that it might take hold of the skirts of the earth,
and the wicked be shaken out of it?

14 It is changed like clay under the seal,
and its features stand out like a garment.

15 From the wicked their light is withheld,
and their uplifted arm is broken.

16 "Have you entered into the springs of the sea,
or walked in the recesses of the deep?

17 Have the gates of death been revealed to you,
or have you seen the gates of deep darkness?

18 Have you comprehended the expanse of the earth?
Declare, if you know all this.

¹⁹ "Where is the way to the dwelling of light,
and where is the place of darkness,
²⁰ that you may take it to its territory
and that you may discern the paths to its home?
²¹ You know, for you were born then,
and the number of your days is great!
²² "Have you entered the storehouses of the snow,
or have you seen the storehouses of the hail,
²³ which I have reserved for the time of trouble,
for the day of battle and war?
²⁴ What is the way to the place where the light is distributed,
or where the east wind is scattered upon the earth?
²⁵ "Who has cleft a channel for the torrents of rain
and a way for the thunderbolt,
²⁶ to bring rain on a land where no man is,
on the desert in which there is no man,
²⁷ to satisfy the waste and desolate land,
and to make the ground sprout with grass?
²⁸ "Has the rain a father,
or who has begotten the drops of dew?
²⁹ From whose womb did the ice come forth,
and who has given birth to the frost of heaven?
³⁰ The waters become hard like stone,
and the face of the deep is frozen.
³¹ "Can you bind the chains of the Pleiades
or loose the cords of Orion?
³² Can you lead forth the Mazzaroth in their season,
or can you guide the Bear with its children?
³³ Do you know the ordinances of the heavens?
Can you establish their rule on the earth?
³⁴ "Can you lift up your voice to the clouds,
that a flood of waters may cover you?
³⁵ Can you send forth lightnings, that they may go
and say to you, 'Here we are'?
³⁶ Who has put wisdom in the inward parts
or given understanding to the mind?
³⁷ Who can number the clouds by wisdom?
Or who can tilt the waterskins of the heavens,
³⁸ when the dust runs into a mass
and the clods stick fast together?

39   *"Can you hunt the prey for the lion,*
or satisfy the appetite of the young lions,
   40   *when they crouch in their dens*
or lie in wait in their thicket?
   41   *Who provides for the raven its prey,*
when its young ones cry to God for help, and wander about for lack of food?

39 *"Do you know when the mountain goats give birth?*
Do you observe the calving of the does?
   2   *Can you number the months that they fulfill,*
and do you know the time when they give birth,
   3   *when they crouch, bring forth their offspring,*
and are delivered of their young?
   4   *Their young ones become strong; they grow up in the open;*
they go out and do not return to them.
   5   *"Who has let the wild donkey go free?*
Who has loosed the bonds of the swift donkey,
   6   *to whom I have given the arid plain for his home*
and the salt land for his dwelling place?
   7   *He scorns the tumult of the city;*
he hears not the shouts of the driver.
   8   *He ranges the mountains as his pasture,*
and he searches after every green thing.
   9   *"Is the wild ox willing to serve you?*
Will he spend the night at your manger?
   10   *Can you bind him in the furrow with ropes,*
or will he harrow the valleys after you?
   11   *Will you depend on him because his strength is great,*
and will you leave to him your labor?
   12   *Do you have faith in him that he will return your grain*
and gather it to your threshing floor?
   13   *"The wings of the ostrich wave proudly,*
but are they the pinions and plumage of love?
   14   *For she leaves her eggs to the earth*
and lets them be warmed on the ground,
   15   *forgetting that a foot may crush them*
and that the wild beast may trample them.
   16   *She deals cruelly with her young, as if they were not hers;*
though her labor be in vain, yet she has no fear,

17 because God has made her forget wisdom
and given her no share in understanding.
 18 When she rouses herself to flee,
she laughs at the horse and his rider.
 19 "Do you give the horse his might?
Do you clothe his neck with a mane?
 20 Do you make him leap like the locust?
His majestic snorting is terrifying.
 21 He paws in the valley and exults in his strength;
he goes out to meet the weapons.
 22 He laughs at fear and is not dismayed;
he does not turn back from the sword.
 23 Upon him rattle the quiver,
the flashing spear, and the javelin.
 24 With fierceness and rage he swallows the ground;
he cannot stand still at the sound of the trumpet.
 25 When the trumpet sounds, he says 'Aha!'
He smells the battle from afar, the thunder of the captains, and the shouting.
 26 "Is it by your understanding that the hawk soars
and spreads his wings toward the south?
 27 Is it at your command that the eagle mounts up
and makes his nest on high?
 28 On the rock he dwells and makes his home,
on the rocky crag and stronghold.
 29 From there he spies out the prey; his eyes behold it from far away.
 30 His young ones suck up blood, and where the slain are, there is he."

40 And the LORD said to Job:

 2 "Shall a faultfinder contend with the Almighty?
He who argues with God, let him answer it."
3 Then Job answered the LORD and said:
 4 "Behold, I am of small account; what shall I answer you?
I lay my hand on my mouth.
 5 I have spoken once, and I will not answer;
twice, but I will proceed no further."

SUMMARIZE

One key point that stood out to you from the Job passage.

_____

_____

_____

_____

_____

_____

_____

_____

JOURNALING & MEDITATION

What is your response to God as you read these texts? How does a sharper vision of God's holiness change your perspective on who He is? How does His holiness change the way you view those who are created in His image?

PRAYER

Based on today's Bible passages and reflection on God's holiness, spend 10 minutes in prayer focusing solely on this phrase "hallowed be Thy Name". Repeat and meditate on the phrase several times and let it draw you closer to the reality of who God is and who we are people created in His image. Let your worship be a natural response to His holiness.

DAY 9: THY KINGDOM COME

Mark 1:9-20

⁹ In those days Jesus came from Nazareth of Galilee and was baptized by John in the Jordan. ¹⁰ And when he came up out of the water, immediately he saw the heavens being torn open and the Spirit descending on him like a dove. ¹¹ And a voice came from heaven, "You are my beloved Son; with you I am well pleased."

¹² The Spirit immediately drove him out into the wilderness. ¹³ And he was in the wilderness forty days, being tempted by Satan. And he was with the wild animals, and the angels were ministering to him.

¹⁴ Now after John was arrested, Jesus came into Galilee, proclaiming the gospel of God, ¹⁵ and saying, "The time is fulfilled, and the kingdom of God is at hand; repent and believe in the gospel."

¹⁶ Passing alongside the Sea of Galilee, he saw Simon and Andrew the brother of Simon casting a net into the sea, for they were fishermen. ¹⁷ And Jesus said to them, "Follow me, and I will make you become fishers of men." ¹⁸ And immediately they left their nets and followed him. ¹⁹ And going on a little farther, he saw James the son of Zebedee and John his brother, who were in their boat mending the nets. ²⁰ And immediately he called them, and they left their father Zebedee in the boat with the hired servants and followed him.

PREPARATION

When we pray "Thy Kingdom come..." what is it that we are asking God? Are we praying that He would reign over this world as He reigns in the heavens? Yet, His reign has never ended even after the fall. God reigns supreme over all creation. The answer to this question becomes clearer as we turn to the beginning of the gospel of Mark. When Jesus begins his public ministry he says, "The time is fulfilled, and the kingdom of God is at hand..." (1:15). In what sense is the Kingdom present in Jesus' coming that was absent prior to this moment? The answer to this question will give us a deeper insight into the second petition of the Lord's prayer. Read the following excerpt from theologian Dan McCartney which addresses this very question.

"The answer usually given is that when the reign of God arrives, God exerts his sovereign rule to fulfill his promises by subduing oppressive and unjust evil powers in the world and establishing righteousness and peace on earth.[1] The cross and resurrection and the sending of the Spirit have brought OT promises to fulfillment. Nevertheless, there are still evil powers in the world, there are still oppression and injustice, and there is little peace on earth. So the question—'In what sense does the kingdom begin with Jesus?'—becomes even more demanding. In what way is God's sovereign rule now exercised that it was not exercised before the coming of Jesus?

We should seek a solution by referring to Jesus' sovereignty. In the resurrection and ascension Jesus receives sovereignty, which assumes that in some sense he did not have it previously. Christ is seated at the right hand of the Father now (Acts 2:32-36). He has now received the name that is above every name (Phil 2:9-11). But in what way was he not sovereign earlier? Was not the eternal Son, the second person of the Trinity, sovereign from the beginning?

The answer to these latter questions is that Jesus received the kingdom as a human. Before his incarnation, the eternal Son was not a man, and thus did not rule as a man. Phil. 2, for example, speaks of the pre-incarnate Christ as equal with God. However, Christ received the 'name above every name' and the homage of every knee and tongue only after, and as reward for, his incarnation, suffering, and death. Similarly, Col. 1:15-20 speaks of Christ as the firstborn of all creation because all things were created in him, etc., but he is the head of the church because he is the 'firstborn from the dead...having reconciled to himself all things, whether on earth or in heaven, making peace by the blood of his cross.' Heb. 2:9 states that Jesus was 'made for a little while lower than the angels' so that everything might be subject to him, he being crowned with glory and honor because of the suffering of death. And Rom. 1:3-4 speaks of Jesus being appointed Son of God in power, which, as J. Murray pointed out,[2] is not a declaration of his eternal sonship but his instatement as man[3] to the position of sovereignty.

This exaltation of Jesus as man suggests some explanation for our first question, as to the way in which the 'reign of God' has now come where it was not here before. The coming of the kingdom, the arrival of God's sovereign reign, is not a reinstatement of God's sovereign exercise of power to accomplish his purposes (which was always true). The arrival of the reign of God is the reinstatement of the originally intended divine order for earth, with man properly situated as God's vicegerent.[3]

Footnotes

1 Cf. G. R. Beasley-Murray, "The Kingdom of God in the Teaching of Jesus," JETS 35 (1992) 19.

2 J. Murray, *The Epistle to the Romans* (Grand Rapids: Eerdmans, 1968) 10.

3 The term "man" here is generic, like the "Greek anthropos" or the German "Mensch." Unfortunately, this term has come to be seen as denoting specifically a male human, compelling us to use words like "humanity" or "people" to avoid implying exclusion of humans who are not male. But the words "humanity" and "people" focus on the plurality rather than the singularity which we wish to stress here, and "human" or "human being" stress the quality rather than the identity. Also, I know of no other term that can as easily capture both the notion of generic humanity and the singular representational character of "the Man" Jesus Christ.

> — Dan McCartney, "Ecce Homo: The Coming of the Kingdom As the Restoration of Human Vicegerency." *Westminster Theological Journal 56, Spring 1994.*

TEXT: ISAIAH 9:1-7

In light of the passage above, read the following text from Isaiah and underline the description of the Messiah.

But there will be no gloom for her who was in anguish. In the former time he brought into contempt the land of Zebulun and the land of Naphtali, but in the latter time he has made glorious the way of the sea, the land beyond the Jordan, Galilee of the nations.

2   *The people who walked in darkness have seen a great light;*
        those who dwelt in a land of deep darkness, on them has light shone.

3   *You have multiplied the nation;*
            you have increased its joy;
        they rejoice before you as with joy at the harvest,
            as they are glad when they divide the spoil.

4   *For the yoke of his burden,*

> and the staff for his shoulder,
> the rod of his oppressor,
> you have broken as on the day of Midian.
> 5   For every boot of the tramping warrior in battle tumult
> and every garment rolled in blood
> will be burned as fuel for the fire.
> 6   For to us a child is born, to us a son is given;
> and the government shall be upon his shoulder,
> and his name shall be called
> Wonderful Counselor, Mighty God,
> Everlasting Father, Prince of Peace.
> 7   Of the increase of his government and of peace there will be
> no end,
> on the throne of David and over his kingdom,
> to establish it and to uphold it with justice and with righteousness
> from this time forth and forevermore.
> The zeal of the LORD of hosts will do this.

SUMMARIZE

One key point that stood out to you from the previous passage.

TEXT: HEBREWS 2:5-18

Consider the role of Christ's humanity being emphasized in this passage.

> 5 For it was not to angels that God subjected the world to come, of
> which we are speaking. 6 It has been testified somewhere,
> "What is man, that you are mindful of him,
> or the son of man, that you care for him?
> 7   You made him for a little while lower than the angels;
> you have crowned him with glory and honor,

8 *putting everything in subjection under his feet."*

Now in putting everything in subjection to him, he left nothing outside his control. At present, we do not yet see everything in subjection to him. **9** *But we see him who for a little while was made lower than the angels, namely Jesus, crowned with glory and honor because of the suffering of death, so that by the grace of God he might taste death for everyone.*

10 *For it was fitting that he, for whom and by whom all things exist, in bringing many sons to glory, should make the founder of their salvation perfect through suffering.* **11** *For he who sanctifies and those who are sanctified all have one source. That is why he is not ashamed to call them brothers,* **12** *saying,*

"I will tell of your name to my brothers;
in the midst of the congregation I will sing your praise."
13 *And again,*

"I will put my trust in him."
And again,

"Behold, I and the children God has given me."
14 *Since therefore the children share in flesh and blood, he himself likewise partook of the same things, that through death he might destroy the one who has the power of death, that is, the devil,* **15** *and deliver all those who through fear of death were subject to lifelong slavery.* **16** *For surely it is not angels that he helps, but he helps the offspring of Abraham.* **17** *Therefore he had to be made like his brothers in every respect, so that he might become a merciful and faithful high priest in the service of God, to make propitiation for the sins of the people.* **18** *For because he himself has suffered when tempted, he is able to help those who are being tempted.*

SUMMARIZE

One key point that stood out to you from the previous passage.

In light of today's readings, in your own words write down the significance of the petition "Thy Kingdom come". What are you asking God when you pray this second petition? What does it look like for you to fulfill your proper role as vicegerent in your relationships and at work?

PRAYER

In light of these readings, take 10 minutes to pray through the significance of "Thy Kingdom come".

DAY 10: THY WILL BE DONE

OPENING MEDITATION

Micah 6:6-8

⁶ *"With what shall I come before the* LORD,
and bow myself before God on high?
Shall I come before him with burnt offerings,
with calves a year old?
⁷ *Will the* LORD *be pleased with thousands of rams,*
with ten thousands of rivers of oil?
Shall I give my firstborn for my transgression,
the fruit of my body for the sin of my soul?"
⁸ *He has told you, O man, what is good;*
and what does the LORD *require of you*
but to do justice, and to love kindness,
and to walk humbly with your God?

PREPARATION

Doing justice, loving kindness, walking humbly

As we come to the third petition, what does it mean for God's will to be done on earth as it is in heaven? In one sense, God's will is always being done because He is sovereign in His omnipotence and omniscience. Yet, this petition is similar to the previous one and we deepen in our understanding of God's will when we consider the key role that humanity plays in the proper governance over this world. The prophet Micah reminds us that God's will for humanity is that we "do justice, love kindness, and walk humbly with our God" (Micah 6:8). Read the following passages to remind you what it looks like when humanity is properly fulfilling our role as God's vicegerents in this world, doing "God's will on earth as it is in heaven."

Read the following two texts and underline what it is that God desires from His people.

1 *The vision of Isaiah the son of Amoz, which he saw concerning Judah and Jerusalem in the days of Uzziah, Jotham, Ahaz, and Hezekiah, kings of Judah.*

2   *Hear, O heavens, and give ear, O earth;*

    for the LORD has spoken:

    "Children have I reared and brought up, but they have rebelled against me.

3   *The ox knows its owner, and the donkey its master's crib,*

    but Israel does not know, my people do not understand."

4   *Ah, sinful nation, a people laden with iniquity,*

    offspring of evildoers, children who deal corruptly!

    They have forsaken the LORD,

        they have despised the Holy One of Israel, they are utterly estranged.

5   *Why will you still be struck down?*

    Why will you continue to rebel?

    The whole head is sick, and the whole heart faint.

6   *From the sole of the foot even to the head,*

        there is no soundness in it,

    but bruises and sores and raw wounds;

    they are not pressed out or bound up or softened with oil.

7   *Your country lies desolate;*

        your cities are burned with fire;

    in your very presence foreigners devour your land;

        it is desolate, as overthrown by foreigners.

8   *And the daughter of Zion is left like a booth in a vineyard,*

    like a lodge in a cucumber field,

        like a besieged city.

9   *If the LORD of hosts had not left us a few survivors,*

    we should have been like Sodom,

        and become like Gomorrah.

10   *Hear the word of the LORD, you rulers of* ^z*Sodom!*

    Give ear to the teaching of our God,

        you people of Gomorrah!

11   *"What to me is the multitude of your sacrifices?*

    says the LORD;

I have had enough of burnt offerings of rams
and the fat of well-fed beasts;
I do not delight in the blood of bulls,
or of lambs, or of goats.

12 *"When you come to appear before me, who has required of*
you this trampling of my courts?

13 *Bring no more vain offerings;*
incense is an abomination to me.
New moon and Sabbath and the calling of convocations—
I cannot endure iniquity and solemn assembly.

14 *Your new moons and your appointed feasts my soul hates;*
they have become a burden to me; I am weary of bearing
them.

15 *When you spread out your hands,*
I will hide my eyes from you;
even though you make many prayers,
I will not listen; your hands are full of blood.

16 *Wash yourselves; make yourselves clean;*
remove the evil of your deeds from before my eyes;
cease to do evil,

17 *learn to do good; seek justice, correct oppression;*
bring justice to the fatherless,
plead the widow's cause.

18 *"Come now, let us reason together, says the LORD:*
though your sins are like scarlet,
they shall be as white as snow;
though they are red like crimson,
they shall become like wool.

19 *If you are willing and obedient,*
you shall eat the good of the land;

20 *but if you refuse and rebel,*
you shall be eaten by the sword;
for the mouth of the LORD has spoken."

21 *How the faithful city has become a whore,*
she who was full of justice!
Righteousness lodged in her, but now murderers.

22 *Your silver has become dross,*
your best wine mixed with water.

23 *Your princes are rebels and companions of thieves.*
Everyone loves a bribe and runs after gifts.

They do not bring justice to the fatherless,
 and the widow's cause does not come to them.
24 Therefore the Lord declares, the LORD of hosts,
  the Mighty One of Israel:
 "Ah, I will get relief from my enemies
  and avenge myself on my foes.
25 I will turn my hand against you
  and will smelt away your dross as with lye
  and remove all your alloy.
26 And I will restore your judges as at the first,
 and your counselors as at the beginning.
 Afterward you shall be called the city of righteousness,
  the faithful city."
27 Zion shall be redeemed by justice,
  and those in her who repent, by righteousness.
28 But rebels and sinners shall be broken together,
  and those who forsake the LORD shall be consumed.
29 For they shall be ashamed of the oaks that you desired;
 and you shall blush for the gardens that you have chosen.
30 For you shall be like an oak whose leaf withers,
  and like a garden without water.
31 And the strong shall become tinder, and his work a spark,
 and both of them shall burn together,
  with none to quench them.

SUMMARIZE

One key point that stood out to you from the previous passage.

TEXT: ROMANS 12

I appeal to you therefore, brothers, by the mercies of God, to present your bodies as a living sacrifice, holy and acceptable to God, which is your spiritual worship. **2** Do not be conformed to this world, but be transformed by the renewal of your mind, that by testing you may discern what is the will of God, what is good and acceptable and perfect.

3 For by the grace given to me I say to everyone among you not to think of himself more highly than he ought to think, but to think with sober judgment, each according to the measure of faith that God has assigned. **4** For as in one body we have many members, and the members do not all have the same function, **5** so we, though many, are one body in Christ, and individually members one of another. **6** Having gifts that differ according to the grace given to us, let us use them: if prophecy, in proportion to our faith; **7** if service, in our serving; the one who teaches, in his teaching; **8** the one who exhorts, in his exhortation; the one who contributes, in generosity; the one who leads, with zeal; the one who does acts of mercy, with cheerfulness.

9 Let love be genuine. Abhor what is evil; hold fast to what is good. **10** Love one another with brotherly affection. Outdo one another in showing honor. **11** Do not be slothful in zeal, be fervent in spirit, serve the Lord. **12** Rejoice in hope, be patient in tribulation, be constant in prayer. **13** Contribute to the needs of the saints and seek to show hospitality.

14 Bless those who persecute you; bless and do not curse them. **15** Rejoice with those who rejoice, weep with those who weep. **16** Live in harmony with one another. Do not be haughty, but associate with the lowly. Never be wise in your own sight. **17** Repay no one evil for evil, but give thought to do what is honorable in the sight of all. **18** If possible, so far as it depends on you, live peaceably with all. **19** Beloved, never avenge yourselves, but leave it to the wrath of God, for it is written, "Vengeance is mine, I will repay, says the Lord." **20** To the contrary, "if your enemy is hungry, feed him; if he is thirsty, give him something to drink; for by so doing you will heap burning coals on his head." **21** Do not be overcome by evil, but overcome evil with good.

SUMMARIZE

One key point that stood out to you from the previous passage.

_____

_____

_____

_____

_____

JOURNALING & MEDITATION

Consider this past week, in what ways are you hindering God's will on this earth? What would it look like for you to be filled with the Spirit of Christ to do justice, love mercy, and walk humbly in your relationships? At work?

PRAYER

Take 10 minutes to pray solely through this third petition "Thy will be done on earth as it is in heaven".

DAY 11: DEEPER MEDITATION & PRAYER

Matthew 6:5-8

5 *"And when you pray, you must not be like the hypocrites. For they love to stand and pray in the synagogues and at the street corners, that they may be seen by others. Truly, I say to you, they have received their reward.* 6 *But when you pray, go into your room and shut the door and pray to your Father who is in secret. And your Father who sees in secret will reward you.*

7 *"And when you pray, do not heap up empty phrases as the Gentiles do, for they think that they will be heard for their many words.* 8 *Do not be like them, for your Father knows what you need before you ask him.*

PREPARATION

As we've come to understand the first three petitions of the Lord's Prayer better, we now come to the point where we internalize these first three petitions further. We need longer times of deeper meditation and prayer to allow information to become formation—for truth to actually form and shape us. When we learn new information we say to ourselves, "I never knew that." When information begins to form us we say, "I realize I need to change this…" When we pray and meditate, we look at truth from the perspective of our lives and what's happening both in us and outside of us. We ponder the question, "What would my life look like if I really believed this?"

TEXT: JAMES 1:19-27

19 *Know this, my beloved brothers: let every person be quick to hear, slow to speak, slow to anger;* 20 *for the anger of man does not produce the righteousness of God.* 21 *Therefore put away all filthiness and rampant wickedness and receive with meekness the implanted word,*

which is able to save your souls.

²² *But be doers of the word, and not hearers only, deceiving yourselves.* ²³ *For if anyone is a hearer of the word and not a doer, he is like a man who looks intently at his natural face in a mirror.* ²⁴ *For he looks at himself and goes away and at once forgets what he was like.* ²⁵ *But the one who looks into the perfect law, the law of liberty, and perseveres, being no hearer who forgets but a doer who acts, he will be blessed in his doing.*

²⁶ *If anyone thinks he is religious and does not bridle his tongue but deceives his heart, this person's religion is worthless.* ²⁷ *Religion that is pure and undefiled before God, the Father, is this: to visit orphans and widows in their affliction, and to keep oneself unstained from the world.*

SUMMARIZE

One key point that stood out to you from the previous passage.

_____

_____

_____

_____

_____

JOURNALING & MEDITATION

Read through your journaling and meditations from Days 5-10 and spend a longer time in prayer and meditation today allowing these petitions to form you. What would change in your life if you really considered carefully the significance of the first three petitions? Consider what change would look like in the areas of your 1) thoughts, 2) feelings, and 3) behavior.

PRAYER

Take 20 minutes to pray through each the first three petitions (~7 minutes each). Use a timer to help you gauge the time.

- *Hallowed be Thy Name*
- *Thy kingdom come*
- *Thy will be done, on earth as it is in heaven*

DAY 12: DAILY BREAD

Matthew 6:25-34

25 *"Therefore I tell you, do not be anxious about your life, what you will eat or what you will drink, nor about your body, what you will put on. Is not life more than food, and the body more than clothing?* **26** *Look at the birds of the air: they neither sow nor reap nor gather into barns, and yet your heavenly Father feeds them. Are you not of more value than they?* **27** *And which of you by being anxious can add a single hour to his span of life?* **28** *And why are you anxious about clothing? Consider the lilies of the field, how they grow: they neither toil nor spin,* **29** *yet I tell you, even Solomon in all his glory was not arrayed like one of these.* **30** *But if God so clothes the grass of the field, which today is alive and tomorrow is thrown into the oven, will he not much more clothe you, O you of little faith?* **31** *Therefore do not be anxious, saying, 'What shall we eat?' or 'What shall we drink?' or 'What shall we wear?'* **32** *For the Gentiles seek after all these things, and your heavenly Father knows that you need them all.* **33** *But seek first the kingdom of God and his righteousness, and all these things will be added to you.*

34 *"Therefore do not be anxious about tomorrow, for tomorrow will be anxious for itself. Sufficient for the day is its own trouble.*

PREPARATION

As we come to the fourth petition of the Lord's Prayer for "our daily bread," we hear echoes from Israel's past after the great exodus and deliverance out of Egypt. During their wandering in the desert, Israel grumbled against the Lord, doubting His provision for them. They believed they would die in the wilderness even after God had performed great miracles to free them.

God has promised in His Word that He will provide for all our needs. God knows what we need even before we ask and will be faithful to provide for us.

When we ask for daily bread, it is a reminder to our own disbelieving hearts that He has been faithful in the past to provide good things and that He will be faithful to provide for us in the present and into the future. When we pray this prayer, we have to loosen our delusional sense of self-control and transfer it into His rightful and capable hands. This prayer reminds us of our daily need to place our confidence in God knowing that He will indeed provide for all that we need—physically, emotionally, materially, and spiritually.

TEXT: EXODUS 16:1-35 | BREAD FROM HEAVEN

Read this passage describing the context of God's provision of Manna.

> *They set out from Elim, and all the congregation of the people of Israel came to the wilderness of Sin, which is between Elim and Sinai, on the fifteenth day of the second month after they had departed from the land of Egypt.* **2** *And the whole congregation of the people of Israel grumbled against Moses and Aaron in the wilderness,* **3** *and the people of Israel said to them, "Would that we had died by the hand of the LORD in the land of Egypt, when we sat by the meat pots and ate bread to the full, for you have brought us out into this wilderness to kill this whole assembly with hunger."*
>
> **4** *Then the LORD said to Moses, "Behold, I am about to rain bread from heaven for you, and the people shall go out and gather a day's portion every day, that I may test them, whether they will walk in my law or not.* **5** *On the sixth day, when they prepare what they bring in, it will be twice as much as they gather daily."* **6** *So Moses and Aaron said to all the people of Israel, "At evening you shall know that it was the LORD who brought you out of the land of Egypt,* **7** *and in the morning you shall see the glory of the LORD, because he has heard your grumbling against the LORD. For what are we, that you grumble against us?"* **8** *And Moses said, "When the LORD gives you in the evening meat to eat and in the morning bread to the full, because the LORD has heard your grumbling that you grumble against him— what are we? Your grumbling is not against us but against the LORD."*
>
> **9** *Then Moses said to Aaron, "Say to the whole congregation of the people of Israel, 'Come near before the LORD, for he has heard your grumbling.'"* **10** *And as soon as Aaron spoke to the whole*

congregation of the people of Israel, they looked toward the wilderness, and behold, the glory of the LORD appeared in the cloud. **11** And the LORD said to Moses, **12** "I have heard the grumbling of the people of Israel. Say to them, 'At twilight you shall eat meat, and in the morning you shall be filled with bread. Then you shall know that I am the LORD your God.' "

13 In the evening quail came up and covered the camp, and in the morning dew lay around the camp. **14** And when the dew had gone up, there was on the face of the wilderness a fine, flake-like thing, fine as frost on the ground. **15** When the people of Israel saw it, they said to one another, "What is it?" For they did not know what it was. And Moses said to them, "It is the bread that the LORD has given you to eat. **16** This is what the LORD has commanded: 'Gather of it, each one of you, as much as he can eat. You shall each take an omer, according to the number of the persons that each of you has in his tent.' " **17** And the people of Israel did so. They gathered, some more, some less. **18** But when they measured it with an omer, whoever gathered much had nothing left over, and whoever gathered little had no lack. Each of them gathered as much as he could eat. **19** And Moses said to them, "Let no one leave any of it over till the morning." **20** But they did not listen to Moses. Some left part of it till the morning, and it bred worms and stank. And Moses was angry with them. **21** Morning by morning they gathered it, each as much as he could eat; but when the sun grew hot, it melted.

22 On the sixth day they gathered twice as much bread, two omers each. And when all the leaders of the congregation came and told Moses, **23** he said to them, "This is what the LORD has commanded: 'Tomorrow is a day of solemn rest, a holy Sabbath to the LORD; bake what you will bake and boil what you will boil, and all that is left over lay aside to be kept till the morning.' " **24** So they laid it aside till the morning, as Moses commanded them, and it did not stink, and there were no worms in it. **25** Moses said, "Eat it today, for today is a Sabbath to the LORD; today you will not find it in the field. **26** Six days you shall gather it, but on the seventh day, which is a Sabbath, there will be none."

27 On the seventh day some of the people went out to gather, but they found none. **28** And the LORD said to Moses, "How long will you refuse to keep my commandments and my laws? **29** See! The LORD *has given you the Sabbath; therefore on the sixth day he gives you bread for two days. Remain each of you in his place; let no one go out of his place on the seventh day."* **30** *So the people rested on the seventh day.*

31 *Now the house of Israel called its name manna. It was like coriander seed, white, and the taste of it was like wafers made with honey.* **32** *Moses said, "This is what the LORD has commanded: 'Let an omer of it be kept throughout your generations, so that they may see the bread with which I fed you in the wilderness, when I brought you out of the land of Egypt.'"* **33** *And Moses said to Aaron, "Take a jar, and put an omer of manna in it, and place it before the LORD to be kept throughout your generations."* **34** *As the LORD commanded Moses, so Aaron placed it before the testimony to be kept.* **35** *The people of Israel ate the manna forty years, till they came to a habitable land. They ate the manna till they came to the border of the land of Canaan.*

SUMMARIZE

One key point that stood out to you from the previous passage.

TEXT: ROMANS 8:18-39—GOD'S EVERLASTING LOVE

Read this passage and underline the promises that God makes with His people.

18 *For I consider that the sufferings of this present time are not worth comparing with the glory that is to be revealed to us.* **19** *For the creation waits with eager longing for the revealing of the sons of God.* **20** *For the creation was subjected to futility, not willingly, but* because of him who subjected it, in hope **21** that the creation itself will be set free from its bondage to corruption and obtain the freedom of the glory of the children of God. **22** For we know that the whole creation has been groaning together in the pains of childbirth until now. **23** And not only the creation, but we ourselves, who have the firstfruits of the Spirit, groan inwardly as we wait eagerly for adoption as sons, the redemption of our bodies. **24** For in this hope we were saved. Now hope that is seen is not hope. For who hopes for what he sees? **25** But if we hope for what we do not see, we wait for it with patience.

26 Likewise the Spirit helps us in our weakness. For we do not know what to pray for as we ought, but the Spirit himself intercedes for us with groanings too deep for words. **27** And he who searches hearts knows what is the mind of the Spirit, because the Spirit intercedes for the saints according to the will of God. **28** And we know that for those who love God all things work together for good, for those who are called according to his purpose. **29** For those whom he foreknew he also predestined to be conformed to the image of his Son, in order that he might be the firstborn among many brothers. **30** And those whom he predestined he also called, and those whom he called he also justified, and those whom he justified he also glorified.

31 What then shall we say to these things? If God is for us, who can be against us? **32** He who did not spare his own Son but gave him up for us all, how will he not also with him graciously give us all things? **33** Who shall bring any charge against God's elect? It is God who justifies. **34** Who is to condemn? Christ Jesus is the one who died— more than that, who was raised—who is at the right hand of God, who indeed is interceding for us. **35** Who shall separate us from the love of Christ? Shall tribulation, or distress, or persecution, or famine, or nakedness, or danger, or sword? **36** As it is written,

"For your sake we are being killed all the day long; we are regarded as sheep to be slaughtered."

37 No, in all these things we are more than conquerors through him who loved us. **38** For I am sure that neither death nor life, nor angels nor rulers, nor things present nor things to come, nor powers, **39** nor height nor depth, nor anything else in all creation, will be able to separate us from the love of God in Christ Jesus our Lord.

One key point that stood out to you from the previous passage.

JOURNALING & MEDITATION

What provisions do you need right now? How have you tried to take matters into your own hands instead of trusting God for daily bread? How can this petition bring a greater freedom and help loosen your grip on trying to control certain needs and desires in your life?

PRAYER

As you consider these texts for today, take 10 minutes to pray through this petition, "give us this day our daily bread."

DAY 13: FORGIVE US

Luke 18:9-14

[9] *He also told this parable to some who trusted in themselves that they were righteous, and treated others with contempt:* [10] *"Two men went up into the temple to pray, one a Pharisee and the other a tax collector.* [11] *The Pharisee, standing by himself, prayed thus: 'God, I thank you that I am not like other men, extortioners, unjust, adulterers, or even like this tax collector.* [12] *I fast twice a week; I give tithes of all that I get.'* [13] *But the tax collector, standing far off, would not even lift up his eyes to heaven, but beat his breast, saying, 'God, be merciful to me, a sinner!'* [14] *I tell you, this man went down to his house justified, rather than the other. For everyone who exalts himself will be humbled, but the one who humbles himself will be exalted."*

PREPARATION

No one likes to ask for forgiveness. It's an admission of our failures, our short comings, our inadequacies, and dare I say our evil. Yet, because of our disdain for acknowledging our sin, we desperately need this fifth petition of the Lord's prayer to remind us often that we are sinners, debtors, and transgressors. But if we are God's children who have been forgiven of all sins past, present, and future, why the perpetual need to ask for forgiveness? Like the previous petitions, this prayer is more for our sake than God's. When we forget the reality of our sins, we grow proud and attribute to ourselves things that flow from God's gracious provision. We easily become deceived and blind concerning our own sinfulness and when we ask for forgiveness we're brought back into the gospel narrative exposing the deceiving powers of sin. We are not as great or mighty as we often think we are. This petition reminds us that even though sin has lost its ultimate power over us, in this life we are never far from sin, and when we can no longer see these sins we grow hardened to God's grace and our ability to be channels of His grace to others.

Consider these words from the Puritan John Owen, "Sin doth not only still abide in us, but is still acting, still labouring to bring forth the deeds of the flesh. When sin lets us alone we may let sin alone; but as sin is never less quiet than when it seems to be most quiet, and its waters are for the most part deep when they are still, so ought our contrivances against it to be vigorous at all times and in all conditions, even where there is least suspicion." (*Mortification of Sin in Believers*)

For this reason, we need to recognize and confess sin in its particularities and not in generalities. Seeing and being convicted of particular sins opens our lives to greater grace so that when others commit wrongs towards us, we are able to extend a similar grace towards them. Our ability to forgive others is the evidence that we have grasped the depth of our own sins and have experienced the greater grace of God's forgiveness.

TEXT: PSALM 51

As you read David's Psalm of repentance, consider what it means to ask God for forgiveness. What is he thinking, feeling, and doing?

> *To the choirmaster. A Psalm of David, when Nathan the prophet went to him, after he had gone in to Bathsheba.*
> **1** Have mercy on me, O God,
> according to your steadfast love;
> according to your abundant mercy blot out my transgressions.
> **2** Wash me thoroughly from my iniquity,
> and cleanse me from my sin!
> **3** For I know my transgressions,
> and my sin is ever before me.
> **4** Against you, you only, have I sinned
> and done what is evil in your sight,
> so that you may be justified in your words
> and blameless in your judgment.
> **5** Behold, I was brought forth in iniquity,
> and in sin did my mother conceive me.
> **6** Behold, you delight in truth in the inward being,
> and you teach me wisdom in the secret heart.

7   Purge me with hyssop, and I shall be clean;
wash me, and I shall be whiter than snow.

8   Let me hear joy and gladness;
let the bones that you have broken rejoice.

9   Hide your face from my sins,
and blot out all my iniquities.

10   Create in me a clean heart, O God,
and renew a right spirit within me.

11   Cast me not away from your presence,
and take not your Holy Spirit from me.

12   Restore to me the joy of your salvation,
and uphold me with a willing spirit.

13   Then I will teach transgressors your ways,
and sinners will return to you.

14   Deliver me from bloodguiltiness, O God,
O God of my salvation,
and my tongue will sing aloud of your righteousness.

15   O Lord, open my lips,
and my mouth will declare your praise.

16   For you will not delight in sacrifice, or I would give it;
you will not be pleased with a burnt offering.

17   The sacrifices of God are a broken spirit;
a broken and contrite heart, O God, you will not despise.

18   Do good to Zion in your good pleasure;
build up the walls of Jerusalem;

19   then will you delight in right sacrifices,
in burnt offerings and whole burnt offerings;
then bulls will be offered on your altar.

SUMMARIZE

One key point that stood out to you from the previous passage.

53 They went each to his own house, 1 but Jesus went to the Mount of Olives. 2 Early in the morning he came again to the temple. All the people came to him, and he sat down and taught them. 3 The scribes and the Pharisees brought a woman who had been caught in adultery, and placing her in the midst 4 they said to him, "Teacher, this woman has been caught in the act of adultery. 5 Now in the Law Moses commanded us to stone such women. So what do you say?" 6 This they said to test him, that they might have some charge to bring against him. Jesus bent down and wrote with his finger on the ground. 7 And as they continued to ask him, he stood up and said to them, "Let him who is without sin among you be the first to throw a stone at her." 8 And once more he bent down and wrote on the ground. 9 But when they heard it, they went away one by one, beginning with the older ones, and Jesus was left alone with the woman standing before him. 10 Jesus stood up and said to her, "Woman, where are they? Has no one condemned you?" 11 She said, "No one, Lord." And Jesus said, "Neither do I condemn you; go, and from now on sin no more."

SUMMARIZE

One key point that stood out to you from the previous passage.

_____

_____

_____

_____

_____

_____

_____

Are there any sins in your life that you have grown so hardened to or have grown so accustomed to that you don't even bother confessing them? What are the effects of unconfessed sin according to these passages? Why is asking for forgiveness so essential to our Christian lives and witness? Are there particular people in your life that God is calling you to forgive?

PRAYER

Take 10 minutes to pray through this petition, "forgive us our debts as we forgive our debtors."

DAY 14: LEAD US NOT INTO TEMPTATION

James 1:2-18 | Testing of Your Faith

2 *Count it all joy, my brothers, when you meet trials of various kinds,* **3** *for you know that the testing of your faith produces steadfastness.* **4** *And let steadfastness have its full effect, that you may be perfect and complete, lacking in nothing.*

5 *If any of you lacks wisdom, let him ask God, who gives generously to all without reproach, and it will be given him.* **6** *But let him ask in faith, with no doubting, for the one who doubts is like a wave of the sea that is driven and tossed by the wind.* **7** *For that person must not suppose that he will receive anything from the Lord;* **8** *he is a double-minded man, unstable in all his ways.*

9 *Let the lowly brother boast in his exaltation,* **10** *and the rich in his humiliation, because like a flower of the grass he will pass away.* **11** *For the sun rises with its scorching heat and withers the grass; its flower falls, and its beauty perishes. So also will the rich man fade away in the midst of his pursuits.*

12 *Blessed is the man who remains steadfast under trial, for when he has stood the test he will receive the crown of life, which God has promised to those who love him.* **13** *Let no one say when he is tempted, "I am being tempted by God," for God cannot be tempted with evil, and he himself tempts no one.* **14** *But each person is tempted when he is lured and enticed by his own desire.* **15** *Then desire when it has conceived gives birth to sin, and sin when it is fully grown brings forth death.*

16 *Do not be deceived, my beloved brothers.* **17** *Every good gift and every perfect gift is from above, coming down from the Father of lights with whom there is no variation or shadow due to change.* **18** *Of his own will he brought us forth by the word of truth, that we should be a kind of firstfruits of his creatures.*

In the Bible, God tests His people but never tempts them towards sin. The difference between the two is that testing has the goal of strengthening faith while tempting has the goal of destroying faith in God. Yet, when God tests His people, we can be led astray by the strength of our own sins, turning what was intended by God to strengthen our faith into a temptation to indulge in our sins. This sixth petition is a prayer of protection so that our sinful desires would not turn opportunities to strengthen our faith into enticements towards disobedience. We are asking God to help us adhere to His ways so that we would be able to walk through these tests and have our faith refined and strengthened. We often do not grow in our faith because our sins overpower our ability to stand firm in these tests; yet, God's grace is at work to lead us away from temptation and towards the ability to remain steadfast in our love and commitments to Him. Life circumstances and decisions are never simply neutral. They can be opportunities that strengthen our awareness and experience of the gospel or they can enslave us, leading us further away from the freedom and riches we have in Christ.

The following two Biblical texts communicate how God is able to strengthen His people to stand firm in the midst of difficult tests—circumstances and decisions that challenge our ultimate commitments and loyalties.

TEXT: GENESIS 22:1-18

After these things God tested Abraham and said to him, "Abraham!" And he said, "Here I am." ² He said, "Take your son, your only son Isaac, whom you love, and go to the land of Moriah, and offer him there as a burnt offering on one of the mountains of which I shall tell you." ³ So Abraham rose early in the morning, saddled his donkey, and took two of his young men with him, and his son Isaac. And he cut the wood for the burnt offering and arose and went to the place of which God had told him. ⁴ On the third day Abraham lifted up his eyes and saw the place from afar. ⁵ Then Abraham said to his young men, "Stay here with the donkey; I and the boy will go over there and worship and come again to you." ⁶ And Abraham took the wood of the burnt offering and laid it on Isaac his son. And he took in his hand the fire and the knife. So they went both of them together. *7 And Isaac said to his father Abraham, "My father!" And he said, "Here I am, my son." He said, "Behold, the fire and the wood, but where is the lamb for a burnt offering?" *8 Abraham said, "God will provide for himself the lamb for a burnt offering, my son." So they went both of them together.*

*9 When they came to the place of which God had told him, Abraham built the altar there and laid the wood in order and bound Isaac his son and laid him on the altar, on top of the wood. *10 Then Abraham reached out his hand and took the knife to slaughter his son. *11 But the angel of the LORD called to him from heaven and said, "Abraham, Abraham!" And he said, "Here I am." *12 He said, "Do not lay your hand on the boy or do anything to him, for now I know that you fear God, seeing you have not withheld your son, your only son, from me." *13 And Abraham lifted up his eyes and looked, and behold, behind him was a ram, caught in a thicket by his horns. And Abraham went and took the ram and offered it up as a burnt offering instead of his son. *14 So Abraham called the name of that place, "The LORD will provide"; as it is said to this day, "On the mount of the LORD it shall be provided."*

*15 And the angel of the LORD called to Abraham a second time from heaven *16 and said, "By myself I have sworn, declares the LORD, because you have done this and have not withheld your son, your only son, *17 I will surely bless you, and I will surely multiply your offspring as the stars of heaven and as the sand that is on the seashore. And your offspring shall possess the gate of his enemies, *18 and in your offspring shall all the nations of the earth be blessed, because you have obeyed my voice."*

SUMMARIZE

One key point that stood out to you from the previous passage.

But false prophets also arose among the people, just as there will be false teachers among you, who will secretly bring in destructive heresies, even denying the Master who bought them, bringing upon themselves swift destruction. **2** And many will follow their sensuality, and because of them the way of truth will be blasphemed. **3** And in their greed they will exploit you with false words. Their condemnation from long ago is not idle, and their destruction is not asleep.

4 For if God did not spare angels when they sinned, but cast them into hell and committed them to chains of gloomy darkness to be kept until the judgment; **5** if he did not spare the ancient world, but preserved Noah, a herald of righteousness, with seven others, when he brought a flood upon the world of the ungodly; **6** if by turning the cities of Sodom and Gomorrah to ashes he condemned them to extinction, making them an example of what is going to happen to the ungodly; **7** and if he rescued righteous Lot, greatly distressed by the sensual conduct of the wicked **8** (for as that righteous man lived among them day after day, he was tormenting his righteous soul over their lawless deeds that he saw and heard); **9** then the Lord knows how to rescue the godly from trials, and to keep the unrighteous under punishment until the day of judgment, **10** and especially those who indulge in the lust of defiling passion and despise authority.

Bold and willful, they do not tremble as they blaspheme the glorious ones, **11** whereas angels, though greater in might and power, do not pronounce a blasphemous judgment against them before the Lord. **12** But these, like irrational animals, creatures of instinct, born to be caught and destroyed, blaspheming about matters of which they are ignorant, will also be destroyed in their destruction, **13** suffering wrong as the wage for their wrongdoing. They count it pleasure to revel in the daytime. They are blots and blemishes, reveling in their deceptions, while they feast with you. **14** They have eyes full of adultery, insatiable for sin. They entice unsteady souls. They have hearts trained in greed. Accursed children! **15** Forsaking the right way, they have gone astray. They have followed the way of Balaam, the son of Beor, who loved gain from wrongdoing, **16** but was rebuked for his own transgression; a speechless donkey spoke with human *voice and restrained the prophet's madness.*

17 These are waterless springs and mists driven by a storm. For them the gloom of utter darkness has been reserved. 18 For, speaking loud boasts of folly, they entice by sensual passions of the flesh those who are barely escaping from those who live in error. 19 They promise them freedom, but they themselves are slaves of corruption. For whatever overcomes a person, to that he is enslaved. 20 For if, after they have escaped the defilements of the world through the knowledge of our Lord and Savior Jesus Christ, they are again entangled in them and overcome, the last state has become worse for them than the first. 21 For it would have been better for them never to have known the way of righteousness than after knowing it to turn back from the holy commandment delivered to them. 22 What the true proverb says has happened to them: "The dog returns to its own vomit, and the sow, after washing herself, returns to wallow in the mire."

SUMMARIZE

One key point that stood out to you from the previous passage.

JOURNALING & MEDITATION

Are there any sins in your life that you have grown so hardened to or have grown so accustomed to that you don't even bother confessing them? What are the effects of unconfessed sin according to these passages? Why is asking for forgiveness so essential to our Christian lives and witness?

PRAYER

Take 10 minutes to pray through this petition, "lead us not into temptation..."

DAY 15: BUT DELIVER US FROM EVIL

OPENING MEDITATION

1 Peter 5:8-9

8 *Be sober-minded; be watchful. Your adversary the devil prowls around like a roaring lion, seeking someone to devour.* **9** *Resist him, firm in your faith, knowing that the same kinds of suffering are being experienced by your brotherhood throughout the world.*

PREPARATION

This seventh petition is linked to the preceding petition by the adversative "but", connecting our need to be protected from ourselves as well as delivered from the evil in the world. In the original Greek, the word 'evil' is preceded by the definite article, which can refer either to evil or to the evil one. In either case, this petition reminds us that evil exists outside of us and that we cannot be naive to this reality. In our modern, "civilized" world, we can become unaware of the reality of evil around us, leaving us quite susceptible to the malice and devices of the devil. As Christians, we cannot ignore the reality of evil and the evil one. Packer rightly teaches in the following quote how this petition reminds us to be aware and vigilant of the evil that surrounds us and to pray often for the deliverance that the Lord is able to bring.

"Can you yet see your own life in terms of being threatened and endangered by evil of all sorts, and so of needing God's deliverance every moment? If not, believe me, you cannot yet see what you are looking at! You are like a person wandering blindfolded and with ears plugged in the middle of a city street, with traffic coming both ways. Learn from the Lord's Prayer what is really going on in your life, and as you are increasingly enabled to discern the dangers, lean harder on the Great Deliverer. 'Because he cleaves to me in love, I will deliver him'—that is God's promise to each saint (Psalm 91:14). Claim it; it is for you."

- J. I. Packer. Praying the Lord's Prayer

Then Jesus was led up by the Spirit into the wilderness to be tempted by the devil. **2** *And after fasting forty days and forty nights, he was hungry.* **3** *And the tempter came and said to him, "If you are the Son of God, command these stones to become loaves of bread."*

4 *But he answered, "It is written,*

" 'Man shall not live by bread alone,

but by every word that comes from the mouth of God.' "

5 *Then the devil took him to the holy city and set him on the pinnacle of the temple* **6** *and said to him, "If you are the Son of God, throw yourself down, for it is written,*

" 'He will command his angels concerning you,'

and

" 'On their hands they will bear you up,

lest you strike your foot against a stone.' "

7 *Jesus said to him, "Again it is written, 'You shall not put the Lord your God to the test.' "* **8** *Again, the devil took him to a very high mountain and showed him all the kingdoms of the world and their glory.* **9** *And he said to him, "All these I will give you, if you will fall down and worship me."* **10** *Then Jesus said to him, "Be gone, Satan! For it is written,*

" 'You shall worship the Lord your God

and him only shall you serve.' "

11 *Then the devil left him, and behold, angels came and were ministering to him.*

SUMMARIZE

One key point that stood out to you from the previous passage.

In this high priestly prayer of Jesus notice how he prays for his disciples. Jesus understood the powerful tempting influence of Satan and victoriously resisted his temptation, yet He had first-hand experience with the luring enticement of this deceptive and cunning creature.

When Jesus had spoken these words, he lifted up his eyes to heaven, and said, "Father, the hour has come; glorify your Son that the Son may glorify you, 2 since you have given him authority over all flesh, to give eternal life to all whom you have given him. 3 And this is eternal life, that they know you the only true God, and Jesus Christ whom you have sent. 4 I glorified you on earth, having accomplished the work that you gave me to do. 5 And now, Father, glorify me in your own presence with the glory that I had with you before the world existed.

6 "I have manifested your name to the people whom you gave me out of the world. Yours they were, and you gave them to me, and they have kept your word. 7 Now they know that everything that you have given me is from you. 8 For I have given them the words that you gave me, and they have received them and have come to know in truth that I came from you; and they have believed that you sent me. 9 I am praying for them. I am not praying for the world but for those whom you have given me, for they are yours. 10 All mine are yours, and yours are mine, and I am glorified in them. 11 And I am no longer in the world, but they are in the world, and I am coming to you. Holy Father, keep them in your name, which you have given me, that they may be one, even as we are one. 12 While I was with them, I kept them in your name, which you have given me. I have guarded them, and not one of them has been lost except the son of destruction, that the Scripture might be fulfilled. 13 But now I am coming to you, and these things I speak in the world, that they may have my joy fulfilled in themselves. 14 I have given them your word, and the world has hated them because they are not of the world, just as I am not of the world. 15 I do not ask that you take them out of the world, but that you keep them from the evil one. 16 They are not of the world, just as I am not of the world. 17 Sanctify them in the truth; your word is truth. 18 As you sent me into the world, so I have sent them into the world. 19 And for their sake I consecrate myself, that they also may be sanctified in truth.

20 "I do not ask for these only, but also for those who will believe in me through their word, **21** that they may all be one, just as you, Father, are in me, and I in you, that they also may be in us, so that the world may believe that you have sent me. **22** The glory that you have given me I have given to them, that they may be one even as we are one, **23** I in them and you in me, that they may become perfectly one, so that the world may know that you sent me and loved them even as you loved me. **24** Father, I desire that they also, whom you have given me, may be with me where I am, to see my glory that you have given me because you loved me before the foundation of the world. **25** O righteous Father, even though the world does not know you, I know you, and these know that you have sent me. **26** I made known to them your name, and I will continue to make it known, that the love with which you have loved me may be in them, and I in them."

SUMMARIZE

One key point that stood out to you from the previous passage.

JOURNALING & MEDITATION

The teaching of Christ and the New Testament affirms our need to pray against the wiles of Satan. He operates in a deceptive manner and often his deceptive malevolence goes unnoticed in our lives as we fail to name and attribute this evil to him. Christ has given authority to His disciples over Satan and through prayer we can effectively expose and counter his malicious influences. What difference does it make when you consider the possibility of satanic influence in your life and in the world around you?

PRAYER

Take 10 minutes to pray through this petition, "but deliver us from evil."

DAY 16: DEEPER MEDITATION & PRAYER

Luke 11:5-13

5 And he said to them, "Which of you who has a friend will go to him at midnight and say to him, 'Friend, lend me three loaves, 6 for a friend of mine has arrived on a journey, and I have nothing to set before him'; 7 and he will answer from within, 'Do not bother me; the door is now shut, and my children are with me in bed. I cannot get up and give you anything'? 8 I tell you, though he will not get up and give him anything because he is his friend, yet because of his impudence he will rise and give him whatever he needs. 9 And I tell you, ask, and it will be given to you; seek, and you will find; knock, and it will be opened to you. 10 For everyone who asks receives, and the one who seeks finds, and to the one who knocks it will be opened. 11 What father among you, if his son asks for a fish, will instead of a fish give him a serpent; 12 or if he asks for an egg, will give him a scorpion? 13 If you then, who are evil, know how to give good gifts to your children, how much more will the heavenly Father give the Holy Spirit to those who ask him!"

PREPARATION

Jesus underscores in Luke 11:5-13 the importance of persistent prayer. He gives this teaching immediately after teaching them the Lord's Prayer making implications between the prayer and the parable. One way of considering these two texts is that the prayer teaches us what to pray and the parable how. We are to approach God in a spirit of persistent dependence being fully confident that He hears our prayers. Jesus further qualifies how God hears— He is a God who is generous, gracious, loving, approachable and empathetic to our requests.

Often our prayers become perfunctory and we lose a certain consciousness that they are actually being heard. In the absence or delay of a response we revert to ritual prayer or give up all together. We are reminded today that we have a Father that listens intently to all our prayers. No prayer falls upon deaf ears and each time we approach God in prayer we have to allow this teaching to soak into our hearts.

Today, we will apply this to the last four petitions of the previous weeks. How do these petitions change if we understood the heart of our God who hears these prayers? Do you doubt that God actually hears your prayers in the manner described in Luke 11? If so, why?

TEXT: JOHN 14:1-14

> *"Let not your hearts be troubled. Believe in God; believe also in me.*
> *² In my Father's house are many rooms. If it were not so, would I have told you that I go to prepare a place for you? ³ And if I go and prepare a place for you, I will come again and will take you to myself, that where I am you may be also. ⁴ And you know the way to where I am going." ⁵ Thomas said to him, "Lord, we do not know where you are going. How can we know the way?" ⁶ Jesus said to him, "I am the way, and the truth, and the life. No one comes to the Father except through me. ⁷ If you had known me, you would have known my Father also. From now on you do know him and have seen him."*
>
> *⁸ Philip said to him, "Lord, show us the Father, and it is enough for us." ⁹ Jesus said to him, "Have I been with you so long, and you still do not know me, Philip? Whoever has seen me has seen the Father. How can you say, 'Show us the Father'? ¹⁰ Do you not believe that I am in the Father and the Father is in me? The words that I say to you I do not speak on my own authority, but the Father who dwells in me does his works. ¹¹ Believe me that I am in the Father and the Father is in me, or else believe on account of the works themselves.*
>
> *¹² "Truly, truly, I say to you, whoever believes in me will also do the works that I do; and greater works than these will he do, because I am going to the Father. ¹³ Whatever you ask in my name, this I will do, that the Father may be glorified in the Son. ¹⁴ If you ask me anything in my name, I will do it.*

One key point that stood out to you from the previous passage.

JOURNALING & MEDITATION

Read through your journaling and meditations from Days 12-15 and spend a longer time in prayer and meditation today. What would change in your life if you really believed that God heard and answered your prayers? Consider what change would look like in the areas of your 1) thoughts, 2) feelings, and 3) behavior.

PRAYER

Take 20 minutes to pray through each of the last four petitions (~5 minutes each). Use a timer to help you gauge the time.

• *Give us this day our daily bread*
• *Forgive us our debts as we forgive our debtors*
• *Lead us not into temptation*
• *Deliver us from evil*

DAY 17: FOR THINE IS THE KINGDOM...

Psalm 145

1 *I will extol you, my God and King,*
and bless your name forever and ever.
   2 *Every day I will bless you*
and praise your name forever and ever.
   3 *Great is the* LORD, *and greatly to be praised,*
and his greatness is unsearchable.
   4 *One generation shall commend your works to another,*
and shall declare your mighty acts.
   5 *On the glorious splendor of your majesty,*
and on your wondrous works, I will meditate.
   6 *They shall speak of the might of your awesome deeds,*
and I will declare your greatness.
   7 *They shall pour forth the fame of your abundant goodness*
and shall sing aloud of your righteousness.
   8 *The* LORD *is gracious and merciful,*
slow to anger and abounding in steadfast love.
   9 *The* LORD *is good to all,*
and his mercy is over all that he has made.
   10 *All your works shall give thanks to you, O* LORD,
and all your saints shall bless you!
   11 *They shall speak of the glory of your kingdom*
and tell of your power,
   12 *to make known to the children of man your mighty deeds,*
and the glorious splendor of your kingdom.
   13 *Your kingdom is an everlasting kingdom,*
and your dominion endures throughout all generations.
   [The LORD *is faithful in all his words*
and kind in all his works.]
   14 *The* LORD *upholds all who are falling*
and raises up all who are bowed down.
   15 *The eyes of all look to you,*
and you give them their food in due season.

16   *You open your hand;*
you satisfy the desire of every living thing.
17   *The LORD is righteous in all his ways*
and kind in all his works.
18   *The LORD is near to all who call on him,*
to all who call on him in truth.
19   *He fulfills the desire of those who fear him;*
he also hears their cry and saves them.
20   *The LORD preserves all who love him,*
but all the wicked he will destroy.
21   *My mouth will speak the praise of the LORD,*
and let all flesh bless his holy name forever and ever.

PREPARATION

"The doxological ending that many Christians are accustomed to pray—
'For yours is the kingdom and the power and the glory forever. Amen'—
did not originally conclude the Lord's Prayer in Matthew's Gospel. The
best and oldest manuscripts do not have it, and the earliest commentaries
on the Lord's Prayer do not mention it. Neither does it appear in Luke's
parallel prayer (Luke 11:2–4). This doxology does occur in a variety of
forms in many later manuscripts. Although it was not originally in
Matthew's Gospel, it is in line with many other scriptural concepts and
probably reflects early Christian practice of adapting the prayer for
liturgical use in the church, perhaps on the basis of 1 Chronicles 29:11."

— *Michael J. Wilkins, The NIV Application Commentary: Matthew*

As we come to the conclusion of the Lord's prayer, what more appropriate
way is there to end than in doxological praise—acknowledging God's
kingdom, God's power, and God's glory. The prayer closes as it began with
our focus upon God, in His incomparable holiness and His unrivaled
sovereignty. This doxology presents to us both a prayer and praise. Pushing
back against the self-centered orientation of our hearts, it is a prayer
reminding us that all that we do in this life is for His kingdom, in His power,
and for His glory. It is a praise that will be proclaimed for all eternity and we
join this unending chorus in this life as our eyes become increasingly opened

to see the greater and deeper truth of this doxology. Our hearts are freed as we worship and attribute to God all that is wholly due His name.

TEXT: 1 CHRONICLES 29:10-22

Read the following texts, underlining those passages of doxological praise.

David Prays in the Assembly

10 Therefore David blessed the LORD in the presence of all the assembly. And David said: "Blessed are you, O LORD, the God of Israel our father, forever and ever. **11** Yours, O LORD, is the greatness and the power and the glory and the victory and the majesty, for all that is in the heavens and in the earth is yours. Yours is the kingdom, O LORD, and you are exalted as head above all. **12** Both riches and honor come from you, and you rule over all. In your hand are power and might, and in your hand it is to make great and to give strength to all. **13** And now we thank you, our God, and praise your glorious name.

14 "But who am I, and what is my people, that we should be able thus to offer willingly? For all things come from you, and of your own have we given you. **15** For we are strangers before you and sojourners, as all our fathers were. Our days on the earth are like a shadow, and there is no abiding. **16** O LORD our God, all this abundance that we have provided for building you a house for your holy name comes from your hand and is all your own. **17** I know, my God, that you test the heart and have pleasure in uprightness. In the uprightness of my heart I have freely offered all these things, and now I have seen your people, who are present here, offering freely and joyously to you. **18** O LORD, the God of Abraham, Isaac, and Israel, our fathers, keep forever such purposes and thoughts in the hearts of your people, and direct their hearts toward you. **19** Grant to Solomon my son a whole heart that he may keep your commandments, your testimonies, and your statutes, performing all, and that he may build the palace for which I have made provision."

20 Then David said to all the assembly, "Bless the LORD your God." And all the assembly blessed the LORD, the God of their fathers, and bowed their heads and paid homage to the LORD and to the king. **21** And they offered sacrifices to the LORD, and on the next day offered burnt offerings to the LORD, 1,000 bulls, 1,000 rams, and

1,000 lambs, with their drink offerings, and sacrifices in abundance for all Israel. **22** And they ate and drank before the LORD on that day with great gladness.

SUMMARIZE

One key point that stood out to you from the previous passage.

TEXT: REVELATION 7:9-17

9 *After this I looked, and behold, a great multitude that no one could number, from every nation, from all tribes and peoples and languages, standing before the throne and before the Lamb, clothed in white robes, with palm branches in their hands,* **10** *and crying out with a loud voice, "Salvation belongs to our God who sits on the throne, and to the Lamb!"* **11** *And all the angels were standing around the throne and around the elders and the four living creatures, and they fell on their faces before the throne and worshiped God,* **12** *saying, "Amen! Blessing and glory and wisdom and thanksgiving and honor and power and might be to our God forever and ever! Amen."*

13 *Then one of the elders addressed me, saying, "Who are these, clothed in white robes, and from where have they come?"* **14** *I said to him, "Sir, you know." And he said to me, "These are the ones coming out of the great tribulation. They have washed their robes and made them white in the blood of the Lamb.*

15   *"Therefore they are before the throne of God,*
          and serve him day and night in his temple;
          and he who sits on the throne will shelter them with his presence.
16   *They shall hunger no more, neither thirst anymore;*

the sun shall not strike them, nor any scorching heat.
17 *For the Lamb in the midst of the throne will be their shepherd,*

  and he will guide them to springs of living water,

  and God will wipe away every tear from their eyes. "

SUMMARIZE

One key point that stood out to you from the previous passage.

Praise and worship only comes as we live in the light of truth and grace. When the gospel is central in our lives, this doxology reverberates in our hearts because we become increasingly aware of His magnificence and magnanimity. There is a wholeness to our being when we articulate our worship and admiration of our God. Praising God includes praising His creation, which includes those who bear his image.

Praising God releases us to be generous in our compliments of others as every good thing flows from the hand of God. How does life look different when His praise is on your tongue? How does it affect your attitude? How does it affect your speech towards others? What concrete things in your life can you attribute to God in the fullness of His splendor?

PRAYER

Take 10 minutes to pray through this petition, "For thine is the kingdom, the power, and the glory forever." Take time throughout the day and recite this doxology and see the difference it makes.

DAY 18: IN CHRIST'S NAME

OPENING MEDITATION

1 Timothy 2:1-6

*First of all, then, I urge that supplications, prayers, intercessions,
and thanksgivings be made for all people, **2** for kings and all who
are in high positions, that we may lead a peaceful and quiet life,
godly and dignified in every way. **3** This is good, and it is pleasing in
the sight of God our Savior, **4** who desires all people to be saved and
to come to the knowledge of the truth. **5** For there is one God, and
there is one mediator between God and men, the man Christ Jesus,
6 who gave himself as a ransom for all, which is the testimony given
at the proper time.*

PREPARATION

These final three words which we typically use to close the Lord's prayer are
perhaps the most important because they reminds us why we can say this
prayer at all; it is because we are in Christ that we are able to pray this
privileged prayer. Through faith, we lift up the Lord's Prayer in His name
because we are conscious that we cannot offer up this prayer in our own
right, but only under the auspice of being adopted into God's family through
the gift of the Holy Spirit. We have no right in and of ourselves to offer up this
prayer. We can only offer up His prayer because of Christ's sacrifice, and so it
is fitting that each time we conclude the Lord's Prayer, we are reminded of
who it is that has given us this amazing privilege. He rightly deserves all the
glory as He continues to live to intercede for His people.

Read the following passage and underline all that we have received being found "in Christ."

3 Blessed be the God and Father of our Lord Jesus Christ, who has blessed us in Christ with every spiritual blessing in the heavenly places, **4** even as he chose us in him before the foundation of the world, that we should be holy and blameless before him. In love **5** he predestined us for adoption as sons through Jesus Christ, according to the purpose of his will, **6** to the praise of his glorious grace, with which he has blessed us in the Beloved. **7** In him we have redemption through his blood, the forgiveness of our trespasses, according to the riches of his grace, **8** which he lavished upon us, in all wisdom and insight **9** making known to us the mystery of his will, according to his purpose, which he set forth in Christ **10** as a plan for the fullness of time, to unite all things in him, things in heaven and things on earth.

11 In him we have obtained an inheritance, having been predestined according to the purpose of him who works all things according to the counsel of his will, **12** so that we who were the first to hope in Christ might be to the praise of his glory. **13** In him you also, when you heard the word of truth, the gospel of your salvation, and believed in him, were sealed with the promised Holy Spirit, **14** who is the guarantee of our inheritance until we acquire possession of it, to the praise of his glory.

15 For this reason, because I have heard of your faith in the Lord Jesus and your love toward all the saints, **16** I do not cease to give thanks for you, remembering you in my prayers, **17** that the God of our Lord Jesus Christ, the Father of glory, may give you the Spirit of wisdom and of revelation in the knowledge of him, **18** having the eyes of your hearts enlightened, that you may know what is the hope to which he has called you, what are the riches of his glorious inheritance in the saints, **19** and what is the immeasurable greatness of his power toward us who believe, according to the working of his great might **20** that he worked in Christ when he raised him from the dead and seated him at his right hand in the heavenly places, **21** far above all rule and authority and power and dominion, and above every name that is named, not only in this age but also in the one to come. *22 And he put all things under his feet and gave him as head over all things to the church, 23 which is his body, the fullness of him who fills all in all.*

SUMMARIZE

One key point that stood out to you from the previous passage.

TEXT: HEBREWS 2:5-18

As you read this passage, consider how Christ's ministry continues to the present day.

5 For it was not to angels that God subjected the world to come, of which we are speaking. 6 It has been testified somewhere,
"What is man, that you are mindful of him,
or the son of man, that you care for him?
7 You made him for a little while lower than the angels;
you have crowned him with glory and honor,
8 putting everything in subjection under his feet."

Now in putting everything in subjection to him, he left nothing outside his control. At present, we do not yet see everything in subjection to him. 9 But we see him who for a little while was made lower than the angels, namely Jesus, crowned with glory and honor because of the suffering of death, so that by the grace of God he might taste death for everyone.

10 For it was fitting that he, for whom and by whom all things exist, in bringing many sons to glory, should make the founder of their salvation perfect through suffering. *11* For he who sanctifies and those who are sanctified all have one source. That is why he is not ashamed to call them brothers, *12* saying,

"I will tell of your name to my brothers;
in the midst of the congregation I will sing your praise."
13 And again,
"I will put my trust in him."
And again,
"Behold, I and the children God has given me."

14 Since therefore the children share in flesh and blood, he himself likewise partook of the same things, that through death he might destroy the one who has the power of death, that is, the devil, *15* and deliver all those who through fear of death were subject to lifelong slavery. *16* For surely it is not angels that he helps, but he helps the offspring of Abraham. *17* Therefore he had to be made like his brothers in every respect, so that he might become a merciful and faithful high priest in the service of God, to make propitiation for the sins of the people. *18* For because he himself has suffered when tempted, he is able to help those who are being tempted.

SUMMARIZE

One key point that stood out to you from the previous passage.

JOURNALING & MEDITATION

It is comforting to know when we pray we don't pray because of our merits but because of Christ's. Our confidence in our prayers being heard and answered doesn't rest in how "good" we've been in the past few weeks, but it is easy to slip into that mode of thinking. We pray because we pray in "His name". Our prayers can never be hypocritical because we pray in "His name." How does your understanding of prayer change knowing you pray in Christ's name?

PRAYER

Take 10 minutes to pray, knowing that you pray in Christ's name. Pray bold prayers because they come from the one who has authorized you to pray in His behalf. Pray praising God for giving us the immense privilege of praying in His name.

DAY 19: DEEPENING PRAYER

Jude 24-25

24 *Now to him who is able to keep you from stumbling and to present you blameless before the presence of his glory with great joy,* **25** *to the only God, our Savior, through Jesus Christ our Lord, be glory, majesty, dominion, and authority, before all time and now and forever. Amen.*

PREPARATION

We have spent the last four weeks learning more about the prayer that Christ taught His disciples. It is a prayer filled with extraordinary meaning and the Scriptures help illuminate the depths of these truths that can become easily flattened in our ritual. The Lord's Prayer reminds us of foundational realities of who God is and who we are because of the gospel. It reminds us of God's name, God's holiness, and God's kingdom. It reveals our day-to-day needs—physical, emotional, and spiritual. Our prayers should be saturated with the Lord's prayer and the more we become familiar with this prayer, the richer and more meaningful our prayer lives can become, leading us into deeper and sweeter fellowship with God and others.

*Now Jesus was praying in a certain place, and when he finished, one of his disciples said to him, "Lord, teach us to pray, as John taught his disciples." **2** And he said to them, "When you pray, say:*
> *"Father, hallowed be your name.*
> *Your kingdom come.*
> **3** *Give us each day our daily bread,*
> **4** *and forgive us our sins,*
> *for we ourselves forgive everyone who is indebted to us.*
> *And lead us not into temptation."*

JOURNALING & MEDITATION

Consider all that you have learned during these past few weeks studying the Lord's Prayer. How has your understanding and practice of prayer changed or grown? How does this prayer lead you to a deeper knowledge of God and yourself? How does this prayer change you?

PRAYER

Use the entire Lord's Prayer as a model for your prayer time considering the significance of each petition.

Take 25 minutes to pray through each petition (5 min each) of the Lord's Prayer delighting in God's presence and all that He has done for us in Christ.

- *Give us this day our daily bread*
- *Forgive us our debts as we forgive our debtors*
- *Lead us not into temptation*
- *Deliver us from evil*
- *For thine is the Kingdom and the power and the glory forever.*

DAY 20: PRAYING WITHOUT CEASING

1 Sam 1:1-20

There was a certain man of Ramathaim-zophim of the hill country of Ephraim whose name was Elkanah the son of Jeroham, son of Elihu, son of Tohu, son of Zuph, an Ephrathite. **2** *He had two wives. The name of the one was Hannah, and the name of the other, Peninnah. And Peninnah had children, but Hannah had no children.*

3 *Now this man used to go up year by year from his city to worship and to sacrifice to the LORD of hosts at Shiloh, where the two sons of Eli, Hophni and Phinehas, were priests of the LORD.* **4** *On the day when Elkanah sacrificed, he would give portions to Peninnah his wife and to all her sons and daughters.* **5** *But to Hannah he gave a double portion, because he loved her, though the LORD had closed her womb.* **6** *And her rival used to provoke her grievously to irritate her, because the LORD had closed her womb.* **7** *So it went on year by year. As often as she went up to the house of the LORD, she used to provoke her. Therefore Hannah wept and would not eat.* **8** *And Elkanah, her husband, said to her, "Hannah, why do you weep? And why do you not eat? And why is your heart sad? Am I not more to you than ten sons?"*

9 *After they had eaten and drunk in Shiloh, Hannah rose. Now Eli the priest was sitting on the seat beside the doorpost of the temple of the LORD.* **10** *She was deeply distressed and prayed to the LORD and wept bitterly.* **11** *And she vowed a vow and said, "O LORD of hosts, if you will indeed look on the affliction of your servant and remember me and not forget your servant, but will give to your servant a son, then I will give him to the LORD all the days of his life, and no razor shall touch his head."*

12 *As she continued praying before the LORD, Eli observed her mouth.* **13** *Hannah was speaking in her heart; only her lips moved, and her voice was not heard. Therefore Eli took her to be a* *drunken woman.* **14** *And Eli said to her, "How long will you go on being drunk? Put your wine away from you."* **15** *But Hannah answered, "No, my lord, I am a woman troubled in spirit. I have drunk neither wine nor strong drink, but I have been pouring out my soul before the* LORD. **16** *Do not regard your servant as a worthless woman, for all along I have been speaking out of my great anxiety and vexation."* **17** *Then Eli answered, "Go in peace, and the God of Israel grant your petition that you have made to him."* **18** *And she said, "Let your servant find favor in your eyes."* *Then the woman went her way and ate, and her face was no longer sad.*

19 *They rose early in the morning and worshiped before the* LORD; *then they went back to their house at Ramah. And Elkanah knew Hannah his wife, and the* LORD *remembered her.* **20** *And in due time Hannah conceived and bore a son, and she called his name Samuel, for she said, "I have asked for him from the* LORD."

PREPARATION

As we come to the close of this devotional series on the Lord's Prayer, this last day focuses not upon the Lord's Prayer but on its relevance in the whole of our lives. As a whole, these petitions can guide us through all the ups and downs that we encounter each day—including the whole range of emotions. As we have looked through the Scriptures, prayers surface out of particular contexts and when our knowledge of God grows, prayers erupt throughout the course of the day. Prayer is not meant not only to be done at set times each day, but as we encounter the unexpected. There are so many things in our lives that need prayer, and yet we can so easily disassociate these areas with the power and privilege of prayer. When this happens we forfeit the peace and hope that the gospel uniquely brings. Take time to consider today, what circumstances in your life need particular prayer.

TEXT: 1 THESSALONIANS 5:12-25

> [12] We ask you, brothers, to respect those who labor among you and are over you in the Lord and admonish you, [13] and to esteem them very highly in love because of their work. Be at peace among yourselves. [14] And we urge you, brothers, admonish the idle, encourage the fainthearted, help the weak, be patient with them all. [15] See that no one repays anyone evil for evil, but always seek to do good to one another and to everyone. [16] Rejoice always, [17] pray without ceasing, [18] give thanks in all circumstances; for this is the will of God in Christ Jesus for you. [19] Do not quench the Spirit. [20] Do not despise prophecies, [21] but test everything; hold fast what is good. [22] Abstain from every form of evil.

> [23] Now may the God of peace himself sanctify you completely, and may your whole spirit and soul and body be kept blameless at the coming of our Lord Jesus Christ. [24] He who calls you is faithful; he will surely do it.

> [25] Brothers, pray for us.

JOURNALING & MEDITATION

Consider all the things happening in your life right now. Go through this past week and recall significant events, conversations, emotions, people, and issues. Use the space below to list out all the things that come to mind. Feel free to consult your calendar to be reminded of the week.

_____

_____

_____

_____

_____

_____

PRAYER

As you look over this list, choose one or two items that you feel drawn to and pray about those things using the Lord's Prayer. Allow the Lord's Prayer to lead you to see new ways you can bring the gospel to bear in this situation.

As you have finished this devotion formally, apply the Lord's Prayer to new life situations to deepen in the experience of God's love and the amazing privilege it is to be able to pray to our Father in heaven...

ABOUT THE AUTHOR

David H. Kim serves as Executive Director of the Center for Faith & Work (CFW) at Redeemer Presbyterian Church in New York City and is the Pastor of Faith and Work of Redeemer. Prior to joining CFW in 2007, David served as a Chaplain at Princeton University, where he also served as the Founder and Executive Director of Manna Christian Fellowship for over 12 years.

He received his B.A. from the University of Pennsylvania, his M.Div. from Westminster Theological Seminary, and his Th.M. from Princeton Theological Seminary, where his studies focused on the public theology of Abraham Kuyper. Currently, he is pursuing his D.Min. at Fuller Theological Seminary in the area of faith and culture. David has a passion for making the gospel real to life, especially in the context of work. He's written a devotional book that connects the narrative of Scripture to our lives today: *Glimpses of a Greater Glory: A Devotional through the Storyline of the Bible*. He's also the author of *20 and Something: Have the Time of Your Life (and Figure it All Out Too)*.

12157900R00061

Made in the USA
Monee, IL
22 September 2019